Powered By The Universe

Electrify Your Magnet

Mohamed Rahman

WOW Book Publishing™

First Edition Published by Mohamed Rahman

Copyright ©2019 Mohamed Rahman

WOW Book Publishing™

ISBN: 9781688924963

Dedication

I dedicate this book to your soul and your heart. I wrote this to help you quiet that seemingly inescapable noise of modern life, to feel within yourself and become aware of your true purpose. You are, undeniably, a product of the Universe, and for all the education you have had in life, whether you paid for it or not, I invite you to open your mind to that which you may not already know.

I dedicate this book to you if you don't already create your own circumstances in life. I want these words to inspire you to reconnect with that which is greater—I call it the Universe. I respect that you might call it by another name. Whatever state you may be in right now, no matter how dire it may seem, it is my intention that you to come to see your life as a gift and to celebrate it as I now do myself!

With the greatest of love and respect
for you and your current experience,

—Mohamed Rahman

Contents

Foreword

Dear reader,

As you turn the pages of this book, you will have a major understanding breakthrough and realization based on what Moh is teaching you within this book. *Powered by the Universe* helps you understand some of the principles that this world operates by, not only on a physical level, but on a level that's beyond the physical. As you understand what Moh is teaching you and apply those principles, you will find an untapped level and resource of energy within yourself that you didn't even know was there.

Moh's attempting—and not merely attempting, he's practically showing you—how you can increase your energy by understanding the power of yourself and the power of the universe. Not only should you read this book, but you should instantly start to apply lessons that Moh is teaching you so that you start to see and feel the immediate transformation that you are about to experience.

I know from having worked with Moh that the information he is teaching you really does have an impact and you can see that through his own examples. The words he has put in this book, when you do them, will help you to create the transformation you are looking for.

Vishal Morjaria

Award Winning Author.

Who this book is not for

This book is definitely not for you if you have already done the hard work in life and achieved a decent result. You can comfortably support yourself and your family, and you are totally happy about the direction you are taking in career or business. You have it all worked out and you look forward to retiring in thirty years or so. Everything is fine.

It is also not for you if you are already a master of your emotions. You know the inner workings of your mind and how to learn from your past experiences and move on. For sure, it's not for you if you don't want or need to understand this wisdom.

You have been lucky in your upbringing, schooling, education, career, and relationships. You seem to simply attract the right people, money, and opportunities to you at the right times. You do this already. And seriously, that is essentially what this book discusses. You really don't need this book at all if all this is in place!

If you are already leading an inspired life, again, this book is definitely not for you. You know what it is to live in the flow. You create your life as it comes, moment by moment. It's a little nerve-wracking but mainly, it's exciting. You're as enthusiastic about life as you if were a three-year-old all over again. Everything is already simple.

Basically, you do not need this book if everything is already going well for you. Do yourself a favour, save yourself some time and pass it onto someone whom you think could benefit from it or simply leave it in some public place for another person to pick up.

Introduction

Hi there!

Congratulations on purchasing this book. Contained within these pages is a blueprint you can use to electrify your magnet to attract to you the opportunities and successes that you deserve in life. Opportunity is around you always. To see opportunity first you need have a goal on which to train your mind's eye. Your goal can be difficult to keep in mind consistently so you also need to be able to clear your thoughts to be able to see the opportunities that can lead you to your goal. Then you need to develop the strength of mind to go for it. Lastly you need to sustain your action towards the goal. It's easy right? I'm kidding! We both know that in today's society this process is much easier said than done. It is now 2019 and after six years of investing in my mind I'm fortunate to have developed the ability to do this process for myself consistently and to realise my goals. Six years is a seventh of my life so I'm sure you'll agree that is a large enough proportion of my life to have practiced this skill and developed some mastery of it.

I have written this book to teach you this blueprint as I have learnt it for myself and I hope you will benefit from this knowledge too. We are all of this Universe yet for all the science we have learnt as a human race so far, there is still so much to discover. But what if there are forces of the Universe that simply cannot be measured scientifically? As a child I loved science and I went on to study Astrophysics at University College London. During my science training I had my first experience of homeopathy—a field of unscientific holistic healing working wonders on my chronic skin condition. I always liked to understand how things worked from first principles but here was a discipline that truly worked for me but was not founded on scientific evidence. This set me on a path to discover different healing modalities outside of scientifically derived Western medicine.

Twenty years later I have only now really begun to appreciate that I don't have to understand everything first in order to make things work for me. In fact sometimes having too much information closes my mind off to opportunities I would not otherwise have seen or therefore taken. In fact, in recent years, I have learnt to stop thinking too much and to simply go with the flow of the Universe instead. Trust me, it is both more relaxing and more exciting this way!

As you read this book I hope you will learn some new things about why it is that you think the way you do and some strategies and models you can use to begin to attract better outcomes toward you. But don't believe a word I say. All I ask is that you keep an open mind and think about the content and even try some of these strategies out for yourself. What is right for me may not be right for you so you can use this book as an opportunity to learn to develop some sensitivity for what works for you.

Allow me to tell you a little bit more about myself though. I consider myself a perpetual student of life and over my 41 years I've become a master of my own personal reinvention. I have survived serious depression, and having been through the cycle many times and having studied a great many teachers in the personal development space, I realise now how my depression was mainly a result of living a lifestyle disconnected from *that which makes me truly happy*. Think about it. Do you even know what it is that would make you truly happy? Is it a large surplus of money, or is money merely a means that would enable you to pursue something different to what you have right now?

For me I realised that my career wasn't making me happy and my health was suffering as a result. I've always paid attention to my physical fitness and my mental state and these have always been a guide to me. For me my happiness is linked to both my body feeling good and my mind feeling good. Happiness is an internal state. Somehow life was training my focus onto the standard corporate rat-race for money instead of pure happiness, like happiness could only come with the cost of time and work. Deep inside me I knew that for me balancing the rat-race with my internal criteria for happiness were not compatible. The future I saw was one where I'd had less fun than I felt I should have had while I was young, with years of healthful vitality lost to the pursuit of accumulating money and resources. And for what? For an old age with a meagre pension and bricks and mortar and a broken body, now too old to have fun, an old age where all the money I might have accumulated would now be spent on managing my poor health. That's if I had any decent money at pension age at all. This made me feel angry and resentful and I started taking it out on those around me including at work.

As I progressed in life, I noticed just how common a story this is, especially throughout the public sector where I spent my career. Acting out of feeling is in our very nature and look at how disconnected we have become from Nature. As babies we naturally act out of how we feel but as we grow older the more we become trained by our parents, school, the media, pop culture, advertising etc to focus primarily on amassing money instead of good feeling. We trade our health and time as a result. Does this feel familiar to you? Does this sound like it will lead you to happiness in your old age?

I am now fortunate to have found a way to move my life towards something that feels much more purposeful than the rat-race. And because I now prioritise my higher purpose it feels like the Universe keeps unfolding to show me the next right steps. As you can imagine, life is much more exciting now! Of course I still need money, but I no longer trade the pursuit of money for having fun. Instead I live a much more abundant lifestyle.

In my twenties I thought I knew it all. As I turned thirty I thought I definitely knew it all. But now in my forties I think, "Wow! There is still so much to learn!" I have come to regard the Universe as a fractal that just keeps on unfolding. Until my mid-thirties I had fought the natural flow of life, trying to accommodate other people's needs and wants for me that it made me feel really unhappy. Unhappy is unattractive and hence I was both too closed minded to even notice good opportunities as they arose and too weak mentally and wilfully, to really go for my dreams. I was also too unimaginative to have any really exciting goals to drive me toward anything better. Until then my life seemed like a turbulent series of ups and downs with constant focus

4

on what little I had compared to that which my soul truly desired. And I couldn't even feel my desire at all. I was misaligned and thus I found myself in deep depression. It turned out I needed to experience deep depression in order to begin my path of healing and self-discovery that has since transformed my life. Subsequently I now have a deep understanding of my inner workings that gives me immense power and confidence in myself—It's like I have discovered an instruction manual for life that no-one ever gave me before. And that is what this book is really about.

I am grateful that I now live in abundance of that magic trio of money, time and conscious attention. This allows me the space and time to create what I want into my reality and live a life feels good, balanced and in harmony with the Universe. Because I feel good, I attract good things into my life, like a magnet. And in this book you will find out how you too can electrify your magnet.

CHAPTER 1

Your Divine Gift

A few years ago, if I'd read this chapter title, I'd have immediately been sceptical. I am not a religious person and if anyone tried to push anything vaguely to do with religion on me, I would most definitely have pushed them away. Having gained better life experience now, though, I have begun to appreciate how much there is that I really don't and cannot know in my lifetime. For you, I absolutely know that if you make it to the end of this book and begin to use some of the strategies it contains, you will also start to understand how true this statement is for you—and even better, how you don't need to know it all. If you do decide to go further in your journey along this path, I promise you that your life will change so magnificently and so wonderfully that you will eventually want to tell other people this same message too. More importantly, once you truly understand it, you'll know it forever! I simply cannot wait for you to make this transformation and I am so excited for you.

Right now, though, you live a lifestyle in which you carry so many judgements about your past. You have some good memories but mostly, you seem to concern yourself more with the bad ones. Those seem so much louder in your mind, and you constantly go over them in a seemingly endless cycle. You imagine what you could have done in hindsight and consider what you would do instead if the same situation arose again. You imagine what you would say or do the next time you see that person, or they say or do a certain thing. You replay it over and over in your mind and dig into the nitty gritty of it because somehow, it makes you feel better prepared for any future events with the same people. You think it's useful to think this way, but the truth is that it leaves you feeling nervous, worried, and anxious. Because this how you are used to thinking this way this is completely normal for you.

Leaving the mask behind

Only you know the thoughts inside your head. The people around you—your family, your friends, your colleagues, and passers-by—all keep you enclosed in your identity as a decent human being who does XYZ job or plays ABC role their lives. They can count on you to be reasonably polite, to act with a certain measure of decorum, and to tone down your true emotions. You've been socialised to hide your true feelings and mask them.

Even that person, the subject of your painful memory that you want to set right, can count on you to act a certain way with respect to them. It's part of your mask. It's almost like you live in Aldous Huxley's Brave New World where people can count on you to be who they think you are and you can count on them to be the people you think they are. We are all socialised to wear masks in society.

It takes so much energy to keep your mask in place. You don't realise how much, but it affects the very core of your being. But behind the mask and inside your head, you constantly review your reality and calculate your next steps. Each time you replay a memory in your head or you construct or reconstruct a certain scene in your mind's eye, you leave an imprint on your psyche which deepens each time. Go over the same ground enough times in your head and it will begin to affect the way you act in real life. It becomes difficult to maintain your mask.

A very dear consultant psychiatrist friend of mine once told me to stop focusing on and thinking about the negative ideas I had voiced to him. I was in my mid-thirties and at the very lowest point of my life. I'd gone beyond suicidal tendencies and blasted through into creative ways I could do more than simply hurt people in my office. You get the picture. Without going into detail, I was so low that I sought professional help. I knew something absolutely had to change. I was unable to keep my mask on any longer. My true emotions were leaking out into my work and social persona. I was under so much pressure I was unable to keep my true self contained.

The Beginning

So began my personal development journey. Throughout my life, I had already discovered that I favoured talking therapies, so I referred myself into psychotherapy for a second time. I love analysing my mind and my thinking, and during this most hellish period of my life, I decided it was time to go a step further and learn NLP (neuro-linguistic programming).

I really felt like a victim in my job and my life always felt as if others were directing it for me, including my bosses. By this stage in my career, I was a highly skilled and experienced data analyst and a powerful resource for my team and division at work. As someone very proud of my work, I felt that what I did really put our division on the map in our organisation. I always was a resource that *does*, rather than a manager who *delegates*, so this meant that I had a string of managers above me to direct both me and my work. Never before in my career had I felt so much that I was being treated like a soulless machine as in this particular role.

The pressure was so great that I had to push back and refuse certain tasks. But why couldn't they understand? I was always particularly unskilled as a communicator and very openly honest with my emotions, good or bad. This often landed me in trouble throughout my life. I knew my "no" was the correct response to my situation, but somehow, I was unable to express it in a way my bosses could truly hear. I knew NLP could help me with this and so I took my first personal development course.

Surprisingly, more than simply help me with my communication, NLP raised my awareness of my situation outside my own head. From this new and wider perspective, I could see that everyone else in my work environment was also anxious and stressed in their jobs. Of course, I could always see that before, but there was now a different quality to it. If I were to approach someone at their desk for a sixty-second question, I would now notice their demeanour in that particular instant before they saw me and they donned their mask. People's masks are especially convincing, especially in the corporate environment.

Thanks to my newly learnt awareness, I was able to interrupt that moment and consciously notice my colleagues for who they really were—innocent human beings forced by society to do jobs to provide for themselves and their families and afraid that they might not be able to perform them as well as required or better than their competition. All this in addition to their other pressures of modern life—they were stressed enough as it is. And my behaviour toward them simply wasn't helping. So having become aware of this, I realised that a career climbing a corporate ladder could never make me happy personally and I knew I had to leave it behind as soon as I possibly could.

I left this job a few months later in what felt like my first wilful act of self-determination in my life, and I haven't looked back since. It turned out that there was a lot to life I had never learnt and for the first time, I took real responsibility for my happiness. Having now invested in my personal development and found real gratitude for my past experiences, I live a blissful life rarely out of the present moment and ever more aware of the beauty that is all around me and always has been. I now live aware of the abundance in my life and I am able to focus on my health in all aspects physical, financial and spiritual, in a way I was never able to before, which led to my lowest point.

That said, I am still human. When interacting with other humans, I go back to thinking like a human in *human terms*, but the truth is that we are spiritual beings in human form. Generally, we have forgotten what it is to think in *spiritual terms*. For me, though, now that I have recovered my spiritual awareness, if I find I lose it, I can easily find my way back to my blissful present with relative ease, and so will you also be able to eventually.

A child is born

When you were born into this world, you were a tiny, beautiful, innocent baby with no idea what was happening and perhaps not even a single thought at all in your head. You were a perfectly spiritual being who had taken human form. Your body went from the heavenly, warm liquid environment of your mother's womb into the icy cold open air of the atmosphere in your birthing room. You drew your first breath which was a totally alien experience at the time, and the shock of it made you cry. You might have had a conscious will but you had no control over your body or your movements yet. Crying was simply your body's reaction to the sheer amount of input suddenly flooding in through your senses from the outside world into which you had been born.

Your parents and family kissed you and cuddled you and loved you in the best way they knew how and they taught you to make sense of this new world. You learnt sounds, textures, tastes, and smells while your vision developed over your first three months. The adults in your life cared for you and protected you while you learnt about your body and what you could do with it. You began to roll over, sit up, and make noises, etc. Your parents fussed over your eating, your sleeping, your hygiene, your everything. You had no established concept of day or night and you most likely broke the routine of your parents, but you had no appreciation for this. After all, how could you know? You were merely days old.

You learnt quickly to communicate through crying or laughing, but you were totally dependent on your mum and dad. You needed to eat, sleep, and learn, but the adults in your life slowly conditioned you to the socially correct times for these activities. Your education had begun.

Everything from the language you were exposed to, the family drama happening around you, the people you met, and the toys you were given to stimulate you had the effect of shaping your learning. As time passed, you learnt language and numbers and other foundational conceptual knowledge like shapes, colours, and sounds. Eventually, you were taken to a nursery school where you played with other children your own age and you learnt the social skills to coexist in harmony with others like compassion, sharing, giving, and respecting.

There were also some painful lessons throughout this whole time which resulted in unpleasantly raised voices or perhaps worse, and these moments especially shaped your thinking and your subsequent existence. Daniel Kahneman in his book *Thinking, Fast and Slow* details how negative experiences have substantially more influence over you than positive ones. Hence, each time you survived a rude awakening, it would shape your behaviour from then on. You learnt the concepts of good and bad.

As you grew up, you went to school and your life grew richer in experience. Your learning became more directed as you grew older. Crying and laughing to express your emotions developed to vocalise the names and other words, and from there, you learned to speak, read, and write. These matured into the more nuanced complex communication skills you now employ in life. Numbers became arithmetic,

arithmetic became maths, maths became calculus, etc. Shapes and colours led to painting which in turn led to art—you get the picture. If you were fortunate enough to have gone to university, you became more and more specialised as your education focus became narrower and narrower. The work grew more difficult but life was generally fun. You were so optimistic for the future and for what would come of your life.

Finally, your years of study and hard work were behind you. You were excited to take life on and claim your independence as a true adult and boy, did you intend to fly! You were now free to earn money and having entered the workforce for your first full-time reasonably permanent job, you could now party even harder, backed with all the money you now made. You had a whale of a time with your friends, your lovers, the parties, the festivals, the adventures, the holidays, the artistic projects, and the collaborations, and you could fund it all. Life was truly a blast. You were barely out of your teenage years and you felt like you knew it all. You weren't even close to your prime.

So what changed?

In your early twenties, five years was a quarter of your life. Fast forward another twenty years, and five years seems only half as long. If you have ever felt like time passes quickly, this is because you have a greater library of memories now than you did when you were a child.

Over the years, the optimism of youth faded as you added another lifetime's worth of experience of professional life and personal responsibilities to your memories. Where learning your job and meeting new colleagues was once an exciting new opportunity, those memories are now old and dulled in comparison to the fresh memories you made of your most recent commute this morning, the unfair deadlines you're facing, the never-ending mountain of work and bills, the difficulties of working with certain colleagues, and even, sometimes, the frustrations at your own family.

Your happy-go-lucky youth is over and is now a long-forgotten memory. You wake one day and realise you never wanted your life to be this way. You used to go through life with a permanent grin on your face. It was so noticeable, random strangers would compliment you. Now, your colleagues catch you concentrating at your desk and they think you look angry. You act differently to how you did as a youth. You reminisce and wish you could go back to that time when things were simpler and you had less responsibility. You dislike who you've become and you feel like you've wasted your prime chasing false dreams and unfulfilling material possessions.

You might not realise it yet, but you regularly take steps to numb yourself. There's a reason why retail therapy and impulse-buying feels good and why you desire certain objects and experiences and people. The same applies to certain foods and drinks, drugs, alcohol, and cigarettes, sex and dancing, sugar and candy, and crack, caffeine, and pills. All have a certain addictive appeal in modern life. Even your smartphone gives you the same buzz when you make the notifications go away or you get likes and appreciation and adulation and recognition. You have unknowingly become an addict.

A frog placed in a pan of boiling water will immediately

jump out to safety to avoid being boiled alive. A frog placed in a pan of cool water and slowly brought to the boil will not notice that its surroundings have become too uncomfortable to bear and it will remain there until it is boiled alive.

Why do you numb yourself what are you numbing?

Everything you want in life at this moment and everything you have ever wanted has been as a result of someone showing you that your life would be better in some way with that thing. Whether the effect is long term or short term is irrelevant. This is why you might drink to excess even though you know its potential cost to your health. So why do you put yourself through it? Could it be that for the short time you experience the buzz, you forget those trials and tribulations of the current state of your life? But why would you want to forget? Could it perhaps be that you actually associate some pain to your current life circumstances? And even if you do have some physical ailment now, perhaps that ailment itself serves a purpose to distract you from the psychological checkmate situation you feel trapped in right now? Think about it.

Pain is a symptom, a warning sign that the current situation is putting undue stress on your system. It's a sign that you are working beyond your tolerance in some way. In our modern society, we tend to mask the pain rather than tackle the root of it—the fact that we are operating outside of tolerance. You have to pay for your necessities in life. You have bills and debts and every year, your money becomes worth less and less. Not to that mention that you also deserve to spend a little to enjoy your life. But you have to work for money. You swap your time and mental energy for a pay packet that allows you to maintain this status quo. In the meantime, you are told to want a nicer TV or car, to buy branded clothes, to purchase the latest smartphone, etc. If you don't want these things, maybe you want to provide them for your family or children.

First, there was the print media and then billboards, TV, and now with smartphones, they literally have you by the palm of your hand. You are constantly bombarded with advertising telling you all the ways your life is not good enough and how you can rectify it. But you can never reach a constantly changing ideal and instead, life becomes more and more painful as a result. So you indulge. A cake here, a drink there, coffee to keep you awake, sleeping pills to help you sleep, and all the other things that bring release as applies to you.

But this pain is not a physical pain and you don't feel it with your senses. It's more that you simply feel down. You laugh about it with others and drown your sorrows with your friends who all identify because they go through much the same as you. In fact, to share with your friends is a kind of release in itself. But eventually, you become a broken record and whine constantly about the same old things over and over. Your friends either tolerate you or they begin to avoid you, unless you provide the same sounding board for them. The 1970's Rat Park experiment and subsequent research might have alluded to the fact that when we feel isolated, we tend to seek relief through our addictive behaviours and indulgences.

But if you have friends and colleagues and other social

interactions in life, how can you ever really feel isolated? Can you ever really be alone anywhere anymore, and especially in the city? But this isolation is more than simply physical and social. This is the pain of the mask you have to bear. This sense of isolation is derived from playing your part in the machine of modern society as you have been educated, conditioned, and socialised since birth to do. You interact and operate as you're supposed to but you're really a robot who is forced into a hole and pushed to provide the service you do. If you don't, then who else will? You're either pushed into it because you are shackled to your bills and need the money or you have to maintain your social status quo. It is an intricate web of thinking and politics—what will this person or that person think, etc. It is the pain of constantly living your life in your ego. The brutal reality is that your ego is anything but connected to your spirit.

Your gift

Your gift is the you who lies behind your mask. It is in all the pain you have stored away in the closet at the back of your mind and all the wrongs and harm others have put you through in life. Your gift is in all the challenges you have faced and obstacles you overcame to become the you whom you are today. It is in your life from your earliest childhood experiences and your upbringing, education, interests, and your professional experiences. Your gift is you. It always has been and always will be. Everything that has happened in your life has happened for a reason. You might not know it or understand it yet. You might have survived horrific abuse or other great ordeals, but these things are your gift—your life experience. And when you live your life giving of your gift, that is when you will live free of the pain of the mask you bear.

Pain is a great motivator as long as you make the decision to overcome it rather than let it win. Most people will take actions to avoid pain and tragically, there are some who will give in and even choose to end their lives because of it. This is not you. If you were contemplating such a course of action, you would not read this book. On the off-chance that you are, I can absolutely guarantee that you have all the resources you need within you to overcome your pain if you choose to do so. If it really is so great, what if this painful circumstance is actually the pivotal challenge from which you can really transform your life?

Exactly like every other experience of life, pain in every form is a gift if you know how to read it. Pain always carries a message that requires you to attend to it to understand its cause. In your mind-body, pain is an unconscious manifestation to alert your conscious mind to something that's not right. To make this book easier to follow lets define some different types of pain.

Types of pain—The traffic light system

Red

If you have experienced the pain of a broken bone or severely torn muscles or ligaments, etc., you will know that this type of pain is excruciating and debilitating. You *may* be able to carry on with the task at hand. In reality, though, you know deep down that your body is protesting and telling you to stop what you were doing immediately and take some action to remedy the pain as quickly as possible. The mind and body are amazing, and there are stories of individuals who accomplish heroic tasks under such extreme pain and usually, these stories show how the person had somehow shut down the pain enough to get them through the emergency at hand. This may happen under drastic conditions but generally, you know that excruciating pain is your body telling you to stop. Expressed as a traffic light colour, this pain could be classified as red—in this context, red is the colour of danger.

Green

So what would be a green sort of pain? One that says go? In the modern world and especially in developed nations, we lead very sedentary, protected, and comparatively luxurious lives. We generally have plenty of opportunity to sit down for much of the day when we are not asleep. For those who don't make it a habit to exercise their body and consciously eat to support their health, we're used to the prevalence of convenience and fast foods. These foods contain high calories and have limited nutritional value. We might even be addicted to their high sugar and caffeine content without even knowing it.

A person who maintains this lifestyle for long enough will eventually need desk adjustments at work, will probably need more and more prescription medicines as life progresses and, somewhat remarkably, will be labelled "comfortable" in their lifestyle. Like the frog mentioned earlier, you may not have noticed it before because this might be a description of what has become your sense of normal. In reality, people who live this way are in a level of pain that they now systematically manage. They will take caffeine, ibuprofen, Valium, etc. As a traffic light colour, this pain could be expressed as green—it is tolerable.

Yellow

This is pain associated with healthy growth. It could be the normal growing pains of a child progressing towards adulthood or the pain of an experienced bodybuilder ripping his muscles in order to rebuild and grow bigger in a responsible fashion. He knows what he can endure and when to stop. I personally have experience of high intensity training and I often experience pains that warn me to take it easy and pay attention to my body or my technique *before I do any real damage*. These kinds of pain can be uncomfortable but are growing, healing, or warning pains. Expressed as a traffic light colour, these pains would be yellow.

How they apply to you

A human in the state of being is a physical body with a non-physical mind connected in some way in a single mind-body system. Just as the body has different strengths of pain ranging from green to red, or tolerable pain to dangerous pain, so too does the mind. And just as the body can grow, heal, and signal warnings in yellow, so too can your mind.

Green is the colour of comfort that discourages people from taking any action because life is perfectly fine and tolerable as it is, even if it is a little dull. They can at least medicate with their vices, be they drugs—legal or illegal—or other vices or escapes including computer games and similar outlets to fiction. If you disagree with this point about fiction, ask yourself how much value you really get from consuming these stories as a function of the time you spend. Could you spend this time being more usefully creative in some way?

Red is the colour of the danger zone. This is a place of fear so strong that you seem stuck or frozen in a state of shock. When you are in this place, you perceive danger and react without using your own conscious will. Instead, you shut down and either fight or run away from the danger or both. In red, you either don't have the time to think, or your options feel limited only to fighting the danger or running away from it without conscious direction. If you ever find that you are in red, the good news is that you can always step back into yellow. Red is useful to know where the boundary is between where you can consciously devise creative new options and where you really cannot.

Yellow is the colour of growth and healing and is where a person truly grows. This place is a comfortable stretch from normal ways of thinking and with the right help and sustained effort, activities in this zone eventually change colour to green. The yellow zone is the place into which your comfort zone can expand, simply by staying in it for long enough. If red and green are places of stillness, then yellow is the place of movement and creativity. Yellow is the place of healing from past pains, letting go, and growing beyond. It is the place of being conscious of your circumstances and taking responsibility for your outcomes. Yellow is the place of truly exercising your conscious will in your own direction rather than allowing others to direct it for you.

So where are you in your life right now? Where are you

in business or your other projects? Are you in red, yellow, or green? In other words, are you frozen in fear or moving in the right direction, or are you bored and under-challenged? Are you being manipulated or externally directed by society in some way but you tolerate it because at least you get to drive the fancy car and have the latest toys? Or maybe you don't have time to think and your life is a series of reactions to one thing after another. If you are not yellow and growing, then do you even want to be? What actions do you need to take in order to move into yellow? Remember, growth and improvement is supposed to be an uncomfortable process as well as rewarding. Be gentle on yourself and accept your current limitations for what they are. You have to know your boundaries first before you can do anything about them.

CHAPTER 2

How Information Becomes Knowledge

What do you really know and how would you know if you didn't?

You have now become conscious of your life in a way in which you have never really looked at it before. This is a new awareness of something that had always been there but which was previously buried or shadowed. You know the scale of the Universe so you know that there is an infinite amount of information you don't know yet. You simply cannot know everything there is to know. It's impossible. And as for concepts that have never been relevant to you before, why would you know them? This chapter will show the different states in which information can exist with respect to your own consciousness. See the diagram below.

You know You know	You know Don't know
Don't know You know	Don't know Don't know

Figure 1 - Phases of knowledge

YK/YK

The first quadrant contains the information that *you know* that *you know*. This statement is obvious to you and so belongs amongst the things you already know that you know. It's important to understand that different people know different things. Just like you are a product of your experiences and, of course, all the things that you know are unique to you, so this is true for everyone else. There is also knowledge that is not unique to you, perhaps shared amongst your friends, colleagues, acquaintances, and society in general, etc. Still, your own personal understanding of this so-called *common* knowledge is still unique to you individually and not necessarily common to all.

YK/DK

As well as the things you know you know, there is also the stuff *you know* that y*ou don't know.* For example, let's take your job or profession. As a child, you became aware that this job existed, but you also knew that you had to learn some new knowledge in order to finally be able to take that job on and do it effectively. You were in a state where you knew there was knowledge you needed that you didn't already know.

DK/DK

In this quadrant lies the information that *you don't know* that *you don't know.* To learn this information requires you to consciously step outside your usual thinking to open you up to these new concepts. The information that lies in this quadrant generally doesn't have any relevance to your life, so it stands to reason that you would not know it, nor would you know of its very existence at all. Clearly, this is the quadrant that contains the vast majority of all the knowledge available in the Universe.

DK/YK

This quadrant contains the stuff *you don't know* that *you know.* Or, rather, the things you didn't know you already knew on some level. These are either your natural intuitively known gifts and abilities, or new information you have studied that you have recently come to understand at an unconscious level. This is that place where knowledge resides immediately before that moment occurs when you suddenly consciously understand, i.e. when you know that you know. Have you ever had an experience, perhaps at school, where you noticed that you were particularly talented at a certain subject or technique, far beyond the level of your peers? Some people have a natural ability for maths and for some, it's art or sport, creative writing, or poetry. etc. For me, it was technical drawing. I seemed to have an ability that was lightyears ahead of my nearest competition without even needing to put in much effort at all to understand it. On a physical level, I already had some innate ability for these drawing techniques which, until then, was previously unknown to me.

How information flows through your levels of understanding

For example, amongst other things, I am a Kangen water machine reseller—get ready for a shameless plug. This section does demonstrate how the knowledge quadrants work so please keep reading, but the above parts cover the gist.

Before I came across this machine, I was already alkalising my water with lemon and cucumber and experiencing noticeable health benefits as a result. A friend introduced me to this Kangen machine which for me, at the time, was brand new information. So this was DK/DK knowledge that then became YK/DK.

I searched the Internet for the machine to learn more. Learning can be considered as moving information from YK/DK to YK/YK. As I searched the internet, I came across a few articles about the dangers posed by some water machines, etc. At this point in time, I concluded I would save my money and continue to use lemon and cucumber in my water.

I was driven by my physical health and my finances. Ideally, I want to achieve an abundance of both in my life. As mentioned in chapter 1, our sense of pleasure and pain are disproportionate. We feel the pain of loss far more than we feel the pleasure of an equal amount of gain. This disproportionality protects us from scarcity and of course, this keeps us operating in the comfort zone, or our YK/YK thinking. Note that this protection is an unconscious barrier we put up between YK/DK and YK/YK.

This barrier is especially relevant to how we protect our finances. Especially with money, we tend to feel the pain of its loss strongly and so to spend it, we have to be strongly convinced of the value of our purchase as an investment in increasing our quality of life rather than a wasteful cost. Throughout our lives, society conditions us to spend money on things that bring immediate pleasure or immediate relief. Healing is an inherently slow and gradual process, but we are conditioned to prioritise quick-fix pills and remedies to ailments instead of affording our bodies the chance to rest and recuperate. Too late, we realise that health is actually the most important thing in life to invest in. After all, how can anyone fully enjoy a good life without good health? So, I learnt to prioritise my health first and foremost over anything else. I learnt to really understand what this means on all levels—physical, mental, spiritual, financial, etc.—and I learnt to invest in my holistic health.

In the process, I broke down the YK/DK to YK/YK barrier and instead of stopping at the articles confirming why

I shouldn't buy the Kangen machine, I was open to looking deeper into it. What you focus on expands and I wanted to find out what the benefit of Kangen water was over simply steeping lemon and cucumber in my water, and why the Kangen machine is so much more expensive than all the other water filters on the market. What was so good about it that justified the expense? Simply by being open to finding out more, I found an event later that year where I saw a demo of the Kangen machine which answered my questions and I left that event having purchased the machine.

After almost two years of diligently drinking this water and even travelling with it wherever I go, I am convinced I made the correct choice. Since changing my water to Kangen water, my body has found a vitality that was always in me but had become supressed over the years. As a result, my body feels profoundly rejuvenated and I am thirsty for the water all the time. *Thirsty all the time* might seem excessive to you, but you are of course 80% water. If you don't refresh your body, of course you'll age and stagnate. You're supposed to use your body physically and want to replenish it all the time. However, a lifetime of sitting at work, sitting on your commute, sitting on your sofa, sitting, sitting, sitting and a lifetime of drinking tap water is what you have come to know—YK/YK.

There is, of course, the wealth of information out there that you don't know—YK/DK, DK/YK, and DK/DK. The question then becomes what new information do you trust? The truth is that everyone has a motivation and I write this part of the book to introduce you to Kangen water as much as to demonstrate these knowledge quadrants, but at least I was up-front about it. What about the media, big pharma and big agra and the other big businesses that have the power to influence governments and manoeuvre society—are they so up-front? Are they more concerned about your health or their profit margins?

In the UK, there is a government guideline that your water intake should be around eight glasses a day. If you're like most people, you probably find this excessive. This amount of tap water seems to pass right through you having left you feeling unpleasantly bloated for a while and not much else. Does the government advice and the reality of what your body can handle seem a bit incongruent?

Well, one of the special qualities of Kangen water is how easily it absorbs into your body. As a result, you can easily drink eight glasses of water a day and feel less bloated. Moreover, your body actually wants to. It has cravings for reasons that will be covered later. For now, note that you don't have to *consciously know* the biochemical complexities of how to absorb water in order to actually do it. Your body *innately knows* and this innate *unconscious knowing* is one part of the set of DK/YK information that, in this case, you were born with.

Now I consciously know what the experience of replenishing with high quality healthy water is, i.e. I feel a healthy thirst, I feel clear-headed, youthful, and energised, and I have clear skin and clear eyes, etc. My body innately knows this Kangen water is healthy which is why I experience a constant thirst for it—unlike normal tap water which for most is quite uninspiring. For me, this is DK/DK knowledge that has now become something I know that I know—YK/YK.

Think about what you know

Think about what has shaped your thirst for knowledge and your thinking throughout your life. Do you remember how open you were to new ideas and information when you were a toddler? How does that compare to now? We've already seen how your life experience has been shaped since your birth by the people around you and your education. Throughout your life, you have also been exposed to the news, social media, the general public, and pop culture. As your life has progressed, you have formed opinions of what is right and wrong, acceptable or not acceptable. You know what you will tolerate and you have some sense of your boundaries.

As a child, you were wide open to learning new concepts and hungry for more. Learning and playing were the same thing—they were fun, so you wanted to learn. You had an unshakeable optimism for your future. As you got older, learning became drier and required more effort. The constant strain of studying for exams and tests and all the associated stress meant that learning became more like hard work than fun. Maybe you were academically gifted, but the chances are your career-based learning has now become an activity you have to do to keep up, to earn money, and to pay the bills and whatever you need do to escape from it all. Learning and playing have become separated and you work for the weekend, rather than living for the sheer pleasure of life, and you wonder where all the hours went.

Learning used to be an abundantly fun, playful creative experience. Time flowed by and before you knew it, you had to go to sleep. As a child you used to cry in protest if told to sleep. Now, you can't get enough of sleep. Your life has become a routine of work tasks, life tasks, and friends and family tasks. Time to do the fun things in life seems scarcer as you trade your time for money which somehow also seems perpetually scarce too.

Are you afraid of the dark?

Ask yourself what information sources you consume and where they actually come from in the first place. What sources do you trust for new information? The government? The media? Certain friends? Where you do trust them, what is the reason for that? Or are you sceptical? Again, think about why that is. Notice how your belief system handles these questions. When you do enlighten yourself with new information, do you ever have a sense that it feels good and right, like a gut feeling? What about those places where on some level, it feels good but you have some paranoia? Does this darkness serve to preserve your current comfort zone? Time and money may seem scarce but at least you have what you have. Could it be that the fear of losing the little you have provides enough of a protective barrier to keep you thinking safely within your comfort zone—your green zone—of what you know you know and don't know? If you want to become more conscious of these barriers inside your mind and how they affect you personally, then Chapter 5 introduces the framework of NLP which you can use to observe, interrupt, and modify your own thinking to empower you so you can achieve better results in your life.

CHAPTER 3

Abundance And Scarcity

You need time and money to survive and depending on how urgently you need them, this balance will play an important role in your choices—not only the choices you make but also the choices you even see in the first place. Your limited choice means you are limited in your actions. And, of course, these limited actions limit the results you get back in life.

Therefore, if you see money is scarce, you will feel a sense of urgency to bring in more money and in turn, you will see limited options to immediately generate that money. Your focus has been tightened to a few choices that will satisfy your monetary needs. Because of the time pressure, you unconsciously limit your choice to what you know, i.e. YK/ YK. To explore anything new might take more time than you have, and it seems too much of a risk, so you stay inside the comfort zone of what you know. Life continues as you repeat the same patterns over and over. You are living a scarcity led lifestyle.

Where I was

Between 2012 and 2014, I worked in a job I absolutely hated. I had been absorbed into a central government organisation and it was my first permanent role in that type of environment. This was a move that had come as a result of a recent election and the action they took to wind down the organisation I had previously worked for. I had entered my mid-thirties and felt past my prime which had been wasted in my previous, also ridiculously stressful job.

I was a management information reporting analyst and accustomed to accepting super difficult assignments which required me to work long hours into the evening to deliver on deadlines. I was still below management grade, even though I now had fifteen years expertise. In my personal life, I had become accustomed to huge debt that kept me focused on scraping by month after month. For me to spend more than two pounds per meal on average would be extravagant. I was early to work and exceptionally late to leave and somehow, I wasted all my free time away.

In addition to this, to this I have a chronic skin condition which was unbearably bad throughout my "prime" years. This, along with feeling broke all the time, hating my job, and generally hating my life, kept me single. I've always been a decent-looking guy and women had always shown interest in me, but I had never felt particularly sexy or confident in myself. As all young(ish) hormonal men with Internet access do, I used a lot of "material" to relieve my needs and because of this habit, I was unable to even speak to any women I fancied. I was so secretive about my crushes that people began to question my sexuality. As if socialising wasn't difficult enough for me already, knowing people thought this of me made me feel even worse.

I felt like the world was pitted against me and I hated myself, I hated my life, I hated my job, I hated my bosses—honestly, I pretty much hated everything about my life. I couldn't really see a future for myself. I felt like there were no decent options and I was so low, I wouldn't necessarily look when I crossed the road. And London roads are busy.

Such was the state of my thinking for much of my career. There is so much more to this but you get the picture. This was the lowest point in my life where my pain had become so bad I would either allow myself to be run over or I would have to turn my life around. I was inwardly focused and I felt truly stuck and without options. It was me or it was them.

How this applies to you

In scarcity, you feel stuck in some way in your position in life. This means that your relationships—be they with an internal part of yourself, or external, e.g. your partner, family, friends, neighbours or colleagues—keep you bound into falsely portraying that masked version of yourself which you know deep down just is not the real you. You may feel bound to your career and perhaps unable to free yourself to try anything new. Or you might dream of dropping your job to pursue your passion as an artist of some sort, but it seems so impractical and you feel like any chance you ever had to make your dream a reality has already passed. It feels easier to bear the pain of letting go of the dream rather than to pursue it. At a lesser extreme, you might simply feel despondent and resigned to your current status quo in life and the work required to do anything different simply doesn't seem worthwhile to you. As a result, you prefer to remain stuck. It's more comfortable this way than to make a drastic change.

Notice how this "stuckness" in your status quo is actually a psychological pain. Using the traffic light system outlined in Chapter 1, this is a green type of pain. Also notice how you don't like your condition but you know that you know you don't like it—YK/YK. Think about how this affects your behaviour and what you project outward to others. Do people really like to interact with you or do they put up with you because they have to? Be honest with yourself.

Scarcity is where you deny a feeling you have deep down in your heart to do something awesome. Your *heart* is the source of your dreams for change. Instead, you use your *head*—your logical mind—to justify all the reasons you cannot change. These logical reasons tend to protect your ego, including your own current beliefs and also the identity you project outside yourself to others. If your thoughts are overly concerned with what others will think, you are definitely driven by your ego mind. Your heart and head pull in different directions. This disconnection will keep you trapped in your situation and eventually, you'll feel depressed. If you were not previously aware of this heart and head link, that's because it runs deep in your unconscious mind-body system.

In this depressed state, you will feel like the archetypal *victim* in some way. You might feel powerless to enact any meaningful change. "What would be the point?" you'll think. Thoughts like this will be based on events you recall from the past that carry pain, resentment, and all the things that previously went wrong—all the chances you missed and all the evidence that your life can't get any better. Your inner world view will be full of negative language and low vibration feelings as you open up old psychological wounds and become aware of old pains you have carried all this time below the surface. Your negative filters will imagine a future where everything goes wrong for you. You will extend the pain you dredged up from the past into the future and it will feel awful.

Why subject yourself to this future? In scarcity, you rebound against this projected future, feeling hopeless and resigned, and you will remain stuck in your present circumstance that you already know so well because it is so familiar to you. How ironically named the "comfort zone" is. Also notice that because your thoughts are so focused on the negative, you will tend to realise those negative results in your life. What you focus on expands.

Your comfort zone

Your comfort zone is defined by all the beliefs you have that shape your identity as a human being. These are beliefs about yourself and also those you think others have about you. In addition, you have unconscious programs that automatically maintain you in your current state and the results you get in life. These are your automatic reactions to things, shortcut responses designed to protect you in some way.

Underlying it all is your *personal thought,* i.e. the thoughts of your ego. Within this area of your ego lies all the knowledge you are familiar with—the things <u>you know</u> *you know* (YK/YK) and the things <u>you know</u> *you don't know* (YK/DK). The underlined parts of each pair represent your conscious mind and the italics what you believe about your level of knowledge in any given moment.

Remember, there are also the things <u>you don't know</u> *you know* (DK/YK). By definition, your conscious mind stuff is blind to these, i.e. these are things you are capable of but which you are simply unaware of. Some of these hidden talents and as yet uncovered facts about yourself you might think <u>you know</u> *you don't know* (YK/DK). Note the blurry line here between these two quadrants. Perhaps there are things you think you don't know but actually you do. Think about it.

If you consider practicing a new skill or technique, there is a transition from YK/DK to DK/YK to YK/YK. The only way to become aware of these as yet unknown talents is to shine your conscious light on this part of your psyche. And in this way, you will expand your comfort zone. This is the process of *growth*.

But growth can be painful. Your belief system is personal to you and by definition, it is unfamiliar for you to think any differently. You also have some beliefs heavily ingrained since your earliest childhood and established by events that were significantly emotional for you. These beliefs might be especially uncomfortable for you to address and are, of course, outside your comfort zone. But they are what limit how far you are likely to reach from where you are currently.

For example, in 1954, Roger Bannister of Great Britain was the first man to run a mile in under four minutes. At the time, experts believed it impossible for human being to achieve this. Many athletes had come close but were not able to beat the time. These runners had a limiting belief that it was impossible to run a four-minute mile and so they were only able to come close but as expected, not break the four-minute time. Undeterred by this common belief, Bannister dedicated himself to the task of beating the "impossible time" and famously achieved this on 6 May 1954.

Once Bannister had broken the four-minute barrier, people suddenly saw with their own eyes that such a time was indeed possible for a human being. Of course, this event re-wrote the previous belief. And miraculously, less than two months later, John Landy of Australia beat Bannister's record on 21 June. On 7 August 1954, the Miracle Mile race was held in Vancouver and Bannister and Landy both ran in under four minutes again in the same year.

Since Bannister's historical achievement, more than 1,400 have run a sub-four-minute mile. All it took was for one person to beat the time. Once that happened and the running community believed it was possible, it opened the floodgates for many more to achieve the same record. Subsequent runners were able to reach further than where their previous limiting belief previously allowed them. So, if you can identify your most limiting beliefs and update them, so too will you be able to achieve what you previously believed impossible for yourself. You just have to take responsibility for wanting to do so in the first place.

Your comfort zone is the net created by your limiting beliefs. You unconsciously designed it to protect you from facing traumatic pains you associated with the significant emotional events that have happened in your life. This type of pain is red. Your comfort zone ensures that you prefer to brave the green pain of today rather than face the red pain of your past. The only way to overcome the pain of today is to release the pain of your past. The secret to growth, therefore, is to venture out into the unknown, beyond the pain of your past, and to allow yourself to try new thoughts and new actions and extend the boundaries set by your limiting beliefs. If you can stay with these new behaviours, then congratulations—you have grown successfully.

Welcome in the spirit of abundance and connection

Remember that in late 2013, I was at my lowest point. I was so devoid of any good feelings about my future that I had very little concern for my life in the present. On the surface, I was "comfortable" with a job, a mortgage, food, and shelter but deep in my soul, I had already died. The optimism and excitement I had in my youth had vanished and my life seemed to have become an endless, repetitive cycle like a never-ending Greek hell. I felt overworked and undervalued and at one point in a meeting with my manager, I shouted a retort to her argument.

There is so much more to my story, but after this event, I sought therapy which, while it was amazing, didn't go deep enough for me. I felt it barely scratched the surface. I had experienced some hypnosis and NLP previously and something inside me inspired me to explore these areas more deeply. I found an online course and this was the foundation of all the control I have of my life and of my mind now. Since learning how my own mind-body system works and beginning to take charge of it, I noticed better results in my life, including in my job at that time. I tried some of the strategies I learned and I found I was able to communicate in a much smoother way in meetings and in a much subtler persuasive manner than my previously heavy-handed way.

I became open to noticing how life improved for me. I became more motivated for life in general, both inside and outside of work. My positive outlook had returned. Even better than that, my point of view had widened such that I was able to notice my colleagues and bosses more. As a main contact for many colleagues, I could see how everyone was under significant stress, managers and directors included. In the lead-up to my depression, I had applied for a promotion, but I realised now that I would never find the corporate environment healthy for me no matter how senior I might ever become. A corporate career path could never suit me and could only lead to deep depression.

Learn to truly respect yourself

Respect is internal. To attract the respect of others, you have to show it first. To show it, you must regard those others with respect. This essentially means to only think about them with respect, which means understanding that you only harm yourself whenever you disrespect others. Respect therefore means to forgive others with love and leave the bad deeds in the past. Applied to yourself, respect is to take loving actions that protect you from those negative energies. All respect begins with self-respect. You either practice self-respect or self-harm. Think about this carefully. If you think about a bad memory, who is feeling the emotion you attached to it? Of course, the victim with the ill feeling is you. And the longer you carry the emotion with you, the more you allow it to harm or impede your conscious reality.

For most of my career, I had generally resented my work. I had always generally conflated my work with my bosses and that affected what I thought about them and how I acted around them. Much of the time, I felt massively overworked, hard done by, and disrespected. Fast forward to early 2014 having learnt some basics of NLP, and I had developed greater awareness of my situation. I could now appreciate my managers' points of view. As it turned out, they were simply human beings, too, each with their own feelings! And they were merely getting on with their jobs when they delegated tasks to me. They had sympathy but they also had their own jobs and their own career aspirations and it was actually me all along who wasn't playing my part in the corporate machine.

With this newfound understanding, I learnt to respect my managers. I also learnt to respect myself. I always thought the respect should come from my managers but I had the insight that it was actually me who wasn't respecting myself. I realised I could never be happy working my way up a corporate ladder and it was up to me to change my future. This could not be anyone else's responsibility. As a result, I began to see new options for my future—an independent future ultimately outside the corporate environment. I learned to love myself, love my colleagues, and to have some faith.

In 2014, I quit my career with no future plans and dived head-first into the unknown without a parachute. I realised that unconsciously, I had worked up to this for quite some time and on some level, I actually made it happen. My heart wanted it, I respected that, and I was able to use my head to calculate the actions, make the decision, and do it.

Connect with your soul

Now, it is 2018, and although my faith has been tested a few times, I am generally known as that crazy, happy, smiley, infectious, high-vibe, high-fiving, attractive and many find me annoyingly so but I really don't give a fuck kind of guy. The last professional post I held in a corporate setting was a three-times salary gain and ten-times time gain on the previous post. I am still human but generally, I now have an unshakeable confidence because I know my long-term path is not to progress up a corporate ladder. On the contrary, it's to respect my heart's true desire.

When your heart is not aligned with your head, you experience internal conflict. Your heart tells you what you really want but your head tells you all the reasons you can't have it. Your education and life experience have separated your logical thinking head from your true heartfelt desire. Left long enough, this internal disconnection will cloud your outlook as you become obsessed with the wants of your ego at the expense of the wants of your heart.

Becoming abundance-minded is about learning to let go of this conflict between heart and head, to heal this connection, and to restore a healthy balance between your heart-led inspiration and your practical thinking head. Once you understand that your heart will always win, you'll learn to use your head to work towards your heart's desire rather than working against it.

Connecting in this way can feel a little scary, but don't be put off by your *fear of the unknown.* This form of scary is actually exciting and based on *faith in the unknown.* Instead of creating pain for yourself, you'll create pleasure. Note that to have faith in the unknown is inherently an uncomfortable position to be in. Faith, by definition, is to give up control to something higher than yourself.

Your heart's calling is from your soul. When you live led by your heart, you'll connect with others at this same soul level and meet them with a healthy, loving respect. You'll naturally feel elated, buoyant, and abundant, just like a child, so you'll project this. People will want to interact with you because you make them feel good. It's an attractive quality, more than simply on a personal level, but also in terms of the opportunities you'll start to notice when you truly live like this.

To unlock this abundance requires you to take responsibility for your mind and become conscious of your inner world and your soul. When you take control of your thinking, you will become more empowered to take risks in faith, and you will actually achieve your happiness. You will develop your self-respect by developing positive inner language patterns. And when you get really good at that, you will naturally become this attractive personality. Again, what you focus on expands. If your thoughts are positive, you will tend to attract positive circumstances into your life.

If you are not already living from a place of abundance, ask yourself why. Maybe you think it's not so simple to think differently in your particular circumstance. Why is that?

Are you able to take responsibility for your feelings or do you tend to consider other people's feelings first rather than your own? If so, does this really do you any good or does behaviour actually distract you from addressing some deep-seated pain? It is in these uncomfortable depths where you will find your truly limiting beliefs that lie at the root of your transformation.

CHAPTER 4

Turning Knowledge Into Skilfull Actions

Recap

In Chapter 1, you learnt about how, when you're out in polite society, you have to mask your true emotions and where that behaviour came from. You shed some light on your journey of how you personally developed since birth into the adult you are today, the emotional journey you took from freely expressing yourself to tamping it down for fear of not fitting in, and finally to the mask you have to wear today. Finally, you learnt about some different types of pain and how you can classify them as red, yellow, or green and how yellow is a healthy place for growth.

In Chapter 2, you learnt about how information from outside of you turns into knowledge. You became aware of how there are things you consciously and unconsciously know or don't know and how these might apply to you. You began to question where you get your information from and think about what you can trust or not.

Finally, the previous chapter covered the nature of

scarcity and abundance. You learnt how a scarcity mindset stems from the disconnection between your heart and your head and how this affects your point of view on life. You discovered that abundance comes from realigning your head with your heart, to respect that which makes your soul sing, and to take responsibility for it.

If this makes sense, you will probably feel inspired to create some changes in your life. You might even take action to think more positively about your current circumstances. At first, you'll try, but the truth is that it can be difficult to sustain thinking differently because you have thought the way you do for your entire life. As mentioned in the last chapter, how you think is determined by your limiting beliefs and their roots go back to your early childhood, more often than not. Because you've had a lifetime's worth of practice thinking the way you do, although some instant results are possible in a short time, it's very likely that you will fall back into your old habits. This chapter discusses the different stages you must go through in order to fully absorb any new skill or thinking style.

Consider how a baby becomes an adult driver.

The Competency Cycle

Unconscious Incompetence	Conscious Incompetence
Unconscious Competence	Conscious Competence

Figure 2 - Competency cycle

Unconscious Incompetence (UI)

Imagine a baby that has just been born. Naturally, she doesn't know that cars exist, let alone that human beings are able to drive them. At this point in time, this information is irrelevant for our new-born and so she remains blissfully unaware. Neither is our infant conscious of driving, nor is she able to do it. Put another way, driving is a skill which our baby is *unconscious* of and not competent at—or, in other words, is *incompetent*. The chances are that our baby is most likely transported home in a car. At her age, she would not be conscious of this means of transport, so although she would have some experience of riding in a car, the knowledge that it exists would be unconscious for her and simply not relevant to her.

Conscious Incompetence (CI)

As our baby ages and Mummy and Daddy start driving her around, our little toddler gradually becomes aware that the thing that transports her and her car chair is a car. She has become *conscious* that cars exist, and she eventually picks up also that Mummy and/or Daddy operate it. She herself is still far too young to drive so of course, she is still not able to manage this skill. For her, it still lies in the realm of her *incompetence*. Again, there is no need for our youngster to actually drive so this skill is still irrelevant for her to actually learn.

Conscious Competence (CC)

Our little girl grows up and becomes a teenager of legal age to drive. She has become more independent and the time has come for her to learn this valuable skill. The reality is that she has known for a long time that cars exist, and she may have watched her parents drive and been fascinated by how they coordinate the three pedals, steering wheel, and gear shift to make the car move so smoothly. She learns some theory about how cars work and the rules of the road and takes some lessons with an instructor. In addition, she has considerable supervised practice as she learns to operate the controls in unison to manoeuvre the car as well as attending to her mirrors and the traffic around her. This culminates in her successfully passing her driving test. Our teenager has long been *conscious* of the skill of driving. Now, she has a licence to prove her *competence* for it.

Unconscious Competence (UC)

The young woman we have known since birth now has her driver's licence now, which allows her to drive unsupervised. She is grateful for her new skill and the independence it brings her but is she a fully confident a driver yet? Of course not. She still has to remind herself to mirror-signal-manoeuvre, her gear changes lack grace, she is nervous in traffic, and she occasionally stalls the engine. At first, she still consciously thinks about each gear change and the sequence of the pedals and her general technique. Over time, though, and with practice, she becomes able to coordinate these controls smoothly and *without thinking* about it. Driving is now a skill that is so automatic for our young lady, she is *unconsciously competent* at it.

So far, so good. Now, let's look closer at how awareness moves between each state in the competency cycle.

UI > CI – Becoming Aware

This is a transition from *not* conscious to conscious. It is about information and whether you have been sufficiently exposed to a concept to have become aware of it in the first place. If you are like most people, it takes about seven times for you to be exposed to something entirely new before you feel a sense of familiarity with it. This is the process of becoming aware.

CI > CC – Practice

To move from a state of not knowing how to do something to knowing it reasonably well, you have to practice the skill. Sometimes, you will already have an aptitude for a skill you never knew you had—DK/YK—in which case, your initial level of incompetence is very low, and it won't take much practice for you to become skilful. For the majority of new skills you learn, however, you will have to put in a reasonable amount of purposefully directed effort and practice.

CC > UC – Persistence

To make this particular transition, you have no choice but to practice the new skill beyond the point where it is fun or interesting to you. Once you achieve unconscious competence at the skill, this is the point of mastery. You have become so skilful, you perform on automatic without needing to think about it. In fact, sometimes, you might find that consciously overthinking the practice actually impedes your ability to flow naturally rather than simply accomplishing it. At this point, you can become creative with your skill, knowing you can trust your body to unconsciously perform your set pieces, e.g. a gear change followed by a lane change followed by an emergency stop. Persistent effort leads to mastery.

UC > UI – Complacency

Yes, it's true—you can cycle back into unconscious incompetence again. At this point in the cycle, you are fully aware the skill exists because you have been through the cycle once already. To continue the driving example, imagine you are a driver with twenty years' experience and are so confident that you now regularly speed on the motorway. Or, on some occasions, you almost fall asleep at the wheel. Your skill is so entrusted to your unconscious mind that you become lazy and complacent about the conscious precision with which you once performed the skill. Because this transition happens in the realm of the unconscious, by definition, you couldn't notice it until a rude awakening moves it to your conscious attention.

UI > CI (2nd cycle) – Take responsibility

The second and subsequent cycles to this transition require you to take responsibility and accept the fact that you have to put some more time into improving what you already know. You will have to expend some more conscious effort and practice in order to cycle through to conscious competence again. The good news, though, is that because you've already cycled through at least once, it will usually be quicker for you to revisit the skill and hone your expertise further.

What does this mean for you?

The competency cycle continues over and over.

This book has introduced you to some new concepts that you were previously unconscious of but now, you are aware of them. When you try to change your thinking style to go against your lifelong limiting beliefs, you will need to practice this new thinking consciously until you can release and overwrite the original belief. You need to prove to yourself consciously that your new thinking leads to better results, over and over again, in order to build your new thinking into a firmly set new belief. The framework of Neuro Linguistic Programming can really help you to understand and own this process and is introduced in the next chapter.

CHAPTER 5

Neuro-Linguistic Programming

The name Neuro-linguistic Programming (NLP) comes from the links between our neurological processes (neuro), the language we use (linguistic), and our learned behaviours based on life experiences (programming). NLP was developed in the 1970's by Richard Bandler and John Grinder through modelling the communication patterns, thinking styles, and attitudes of highly successful psychotherapists in their time. They worked closely with Virginia Satir (Systemic Family Therapy), Fritz Perls (Gestalt Therapy), and Milton Erickson (Hypnotherapy). Bandler and Grinder wanted to distil the essence of what made these psychotherapists so special and learn how these specialities could be transferred to other people. The result was NLP, which is a set of beliefs, skills, and techniques which can be used therapeutically to deconstruct your reality to identify and heal old psychological wounds that no longer serve you.

Notice that you experience your reality through your thought processes.

Think about it

Pause for a moment and think about it.

Everything you personally experience in life has only one thing in common. That thing is you. You are the only entity who has been witness to all the events in your life. You exist simultaneously as a human who has been, a human who is being, and a human who is yet to be. But what exactly is this "human" part of your being?

You have been blessed with a physical body with which to observe the physical world around you. Your body has five physical senses of sight, sound, touch, taste, and smell. With these, you take in feedback from the world around you, and all these senses contribute to your sense of "reality."

In addition to your five main senses, you also have your internal thought processes which are either an internal dialogue or an inner visual sense. You probably use one more than the other. Your internal dialogue is the voice inside your head, and your inner visual sense provides the images you are able to picture inside your mind. You are also capable of imagining the senses of sound, touch, taste, and smell. Your senses, your internal experiences, and landscape are all unique to you as are your memories, your beliefs, and your body.

It is well proven scientifically that the true physical reality in which you move your body and interact contains far more detail than each of your individual senses can even handle. This means that there is more to see than your eyes are able to without aid, there are sounds that your ears are unable to hear, etc. For example, humans look into deepest space using telescopes and dogs can hear far beyond the human typical audio spectrum.

All the information that comes in through your senses is filtered through your mind in order to create a projection of your reality. Put another way, the projection you have of your reality is constructed from the information that has filtered in through your five senses. Your perception of reality is a projection which is presented to the part of your mind that is actively paying attention—your conscious mind.

Your mind exists in two parts

Your *conscious* mind is the part of your mind that is your actively focused attention. The other much larger part of your mind is your *unconscious*. This is out of focus but still very much present. The line that delineates both constantly shifts. For example, when you sleep, your mind is almost entirely unconscious.

How hot or cold is the sole of your left foot? The chances are that you were not conscious of your left foot until you read this question. Your foot constantly receives feedback from the environment, yet this information was not passed to your conscious mind until the question directed you to think of your left foot. Before that, the information was in the realm of your unconscious. This exercise shows how the conscious/unconscious line can shift and how you are able to consciously control it if you want to. Almost all your bodily processes are controlled unconsciously. A few examples include your breathing, heartbeat, and pain management. You do not generally think about your breathing in order to breathe. It is generally an automatic, unconscious process although it is easy to bring it under your conscious control.

Your unconscious mind is vastly bigger than your conscious mind. The latter can only focus on 7 ± 2 things in any given instant. It simply cannot perform the tremendous number of functions required to run your human body successfully, let alone your intellectual and spiritual personal life. Your unconscious is significantly more powerful and handles every single byte of information that is gathered by your senses, keeps your body alive, and maintains a filing system for your memories and beliefs. And it does it all at a much faster speed than you could possibly process consciously.

Your conscious focus shifts constantly. This means that as new input is presented to your conscious awareness, one of the other 7 ± 2 things you were thinking about moves back into your unconscious. As an example, were you really still thinking of the temperature of your left foot while reading and pondering this last paragraph? Probably not.

With all of the information that comes in through your senses, it would be impossible to consciously vet every single physical sensation before deciding if it was relevant to your objective or not. You might have a deep conversation with a friend while walking. You'll naturally reserve your conscious attention for your friend, rather than the bodily processes required for walking. If you had to coordinate your muscles, balance, blood flow, breathing, oxygenation, etc., how would you have space to consciously attend to your friend? These processes simply take place unconsciously without you needing to be conscious of them and are hardwired into your physical brain and body.

Your belief system

Between your hard-wired neurology and your flexible conscious processes, you also have automatic neurological programs which you run as shortcuts in order for you to be able to react quickly to certain stimulus. These programs are your beliefs about yourself, your environment, and your capabilities. Many of these act as shortcuts which you developed to protect you from dangers you might come across in your surrounding environment. Let's say, for example, you notice a snake out of the corner of your eye. Immediately, you experience shock and fear only to discover the snake is actually a wiggly stick. Let's unpick some of the operations your mind would run in that one instant.

Unconsciously, your mind would receive an image of the wiggly stick from out of the corner of your eye. Your unconscious mind would compare this picture with other pictures in your memory, culminating in a fear response. Your mind and body would conclude together that your best course of action would be to stop, ready your body to flee or react quickly, and to turn your head immediately to really take a proper look at the object. This would trigger a state of fear as you would have fully trained your full conscious attention toward assessing the possible threat. Following your close inspection, you would conclude that the object is actually only a wiggly stick. Your mind would then add this experience to your personal belief system, ready to access again in future the next time a similar situation arises. Your system would then relax and you would dismiss the object back into your unconscious awareness.

Your unconscious mind constantly compares the input

from your environment with your beliefs. In this way, your beliefs are designed to protect you. Your unconscious always has what it thinks are your best interests at heart, even if that is a response to do physical harm in some way in moments of perceived threat.

Everything you have ever experienced in your life has been recorded in your memory as part of your vast personal, internalised reference library. Every piece of input you have ever taken in through your senses in your life, consciously or otherwise, has been stored in your mind. Notice how this means that far more has been recorded by your memory than you were ever consciously aware of at the time, and that you are able to consciously access it now. Your internal reference library of memories is simply enormous.

As you continue to experience your life, you continue to record new events as new connections in your mind, and the internal network of your memory grows and evolves. As you age, you notice patterns in your memories. For example, Action 1 produces Result 1. The more you do Action 1 and get Result 1, the stronger your association between them becomes. Eventually, you learn to rely on *the fact* that Result 1 will follow Action 1. This *fact* is actually a new *belief* and something you now know and trust to be a truth you can rely on.

A belief can evoke feelings of pleasure or pain, and this will either drive you to perform Action 1 more or less often or even to stop it completely, depending on the strength of the feeling. A core driver of your being is the pursuit of happiness, or feeling good. This might inspire you to think creatively, and given that Event 1 feels so good, you might start to artistically adjust the way you perform Action 1 in order to achieve greater pleasure. You will gain further feedback from your environment and you will create further memories, beliefs, and associations, and your internal reference library thus evolves. The size of your library is unfathomable and yet it is only a small part of your unconscious.

The older you grow and the richer your experience of life, the more memories and beliefs you form. Your beliefs serve as shortcuts to allow you to make unconscious decisions, i.e. to take actions with little or no conscious effort. The longer you live, the more unconsciously competent you become at more tasks and the more likely it will be that you make decisions unconsciously based on your unconscious beliefs. You are no longer consciously directing your life.

How your beliefs affect your outlook

Think of the colour blue.

Move your gaze around your current environment and notice how it will settle on anything blue. After you have investigated everything in your sight and identified everything blue, you will notice other things that are not pure blue but have blue tones and you will start to count them also.

This is your Reticular Activating System at work. The RAS sets your focus and as a result, you will look for confirmation of your focus. The more you look for the confirmation, the more you will find it, because whatever you choose to focus on will always expand as you adjust the requirement—blue, in this case—to include blueish-green turquoise, purples, indigos, greys, blacks, and at a stretch, browns, greens, etc.

Given any suggestion for your RAS, you will naturally and unconsciously *delete, distort,* and *generalise* the input you receive through your senses in order to create a manageable experience for your conscious mind. In the above case, you consult your belief system for what constitutes your idea of blue and *delete, distort,* and *generalise* what you see to match this focus.

For example, around my room as I write this are the following items: a blue tin of moisturiser, a blue tube of ointment, a blue toothpick, a blue power light, and a few other items. These items are all actually blue. I am not looking for anything that is not. This means that as I scan my environment, I ignore anything not identifiable as blue. This is an example of *deletion.*

There are also other objects that vaguely match my personal idea of blue. A couple of clear plastic water bottles with blue tones to them, a couple of clear wine glasses, my dark-grey mouse and its lighter grey lead, my light, silvery-grey laptop. These items are not really blue, but they'll do. This is an example of *distortion.*

I could report that *everything* my eyes settled on was blue or that *all* of the objects are blue or have some component of blue to them. These are statements that demonstrate *generalisation.*

You use these filters unconsciously all the time—did you notice my generalisation there? Deleting, distorting, and generalising are shortcuts that your brain uses in order to process information quickly. After all, your senses gather too much information for you to consciously process in any given moment so you have to be able to quickly sort the relevant stuff from the irrelevant in order to keep up with the pace of life. And life goes fast—faster than you can consciously observe. Remember the wiggly stick. What if it was a dangerous snake ready to attack you? What if you were told that Brian's not the Messiah, he is a very naughty boy? How will that affect how you see Brian? How will that change your behaviour toward Brian as a result?

Some of what you what you have seen in life might have had a powerful emotional impact on you. The more powerful your emotional response, the deeper your memories will cut and the more powerful the beliefs you will form. If you experience an especially significant emotional event or trauma, this will affect how you delete, distort, and generalise incoming information and also, therefore, your future beliefs.

Your memory, like your unconscious, is perfect. Your ability to consciously recall events from your memory is not so perfect, however.

Beliefs and the feelings attached to them not only affect how you encode your experiences, but they also affect how you recall past events. For example, if the memory was of a particularly traumatic event, the feelings associated with it will be too painful to consciously face. In these cases, your unconscious will bury these memories and either hide them completely (delete), or tone them down or soften them (distort and generalise) in order to make them easier for you to consciously handle. As you grow in life, you pick up more resources and understanding. The traumas your unconscious once buried will start to present themselves again when your unconscious thinks you are consciously able to deal with them.

Thinking styles

Your own personal thinking style affects the way you apply your conscious focus. As you read this section, you might recognise these traits in yourself, your loved ones, or other important people in your life. Thinking styles can be described using meta-programs. These can enable you to understand someone's preferences. A few examples of meta-programs are provided below. It's important to note that any individual's preferences may change over time, but most people are usually one thing more than the other.

> **Toward or Away** – You are motivated by pleasure and pain in some way. In some aspects, you are motivated to move toward pleasure, for example a reward in the form of a lucrative bonus. In other ways, you might procrastinate over certain messy or mind-numbing tasks and prefer to do other more appealing tasks instead, i.e. move away from pain. Consider your routine tasks at work or at home. Can you identify your toward and away characteristics? Can you notice how they play out in other people around you?

> **Internal or External** – Are you someone who loves to receive praise and recognition from others? Do certificates from external bodies mean much to you? Or perhaps you know inside you that the work you did was a good job well done and that's what ultimately satisfies you. Maybe you are recognised for a job well done, but you know deep inside that you could have put more effort in and it is difficult for you to accept this praise from outside?

Matcher or Mismatcher – Is there someone in your life who simply has to disagree with every opinion you have? Perhaps they don't express it but you know that's what they are thinking. These people may simply be mismatchers who have to explore the other side of the equation. Note that this is simply an unconscious program they run that serves them well in life. Similarly, there are people who constantly agree with everything you do. As harmonious as this might seem, perhaps these people could be more independent sometimes. Which might you be? Does it depend on the context?

Possibility or Necessity – Your language really does affect the options you see in life. Do you meet life commitments out of a sense of *having* to or *wanting* to? Think about your circumstances. Do you *have* to work because you have bills to pay? This is necessity. Or do you work on projects out of a sense of genuinely *wanting* to? Money flows to you because people find so much value in your work, and you happen to be able to pay the bills. This is a possibility. Of course, this can change in any moment for any individual's circumstances, but do they really *want* to or do they *have* to?

The NLP Communication Model

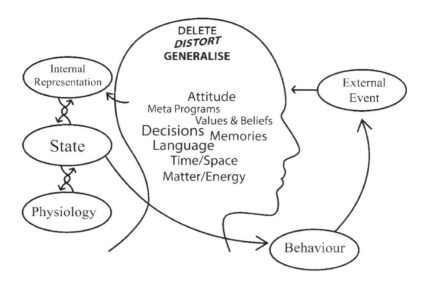

Figure 3 - The NLP Communication Model

In this chapter so far, we have discussed that you have five main senses of sight, sound, touch, taste, and smell. You also have an inner voice and you can use your imagination to picture your dreams, goals, or what might happen in future. You have a part of your mind that you actively use to think with, your conscious mind. And you have another part of your mind that works on automatic, your unconscious. You can pick what you consciously focus on and you can extend your limits of focus.

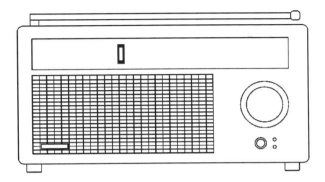

Figure 4 - An old school analogue radio

Consider an old radio set with a knob that can be turned to tune it. The entirety of the frequencies on offer represents your unconscious. Your conscious focus is the band you tune into. Your beliefs and meta-programs are the limits of the radio—these are the stops at the ends of the dial. Your unconscious awareness is the total frequency range of the radio and your conscious focus is the small channel of 7 ± 2 things you are tuned into. The tuning control knob represents your RAS. The more you grow spiritually, the wider the stops at the ends of the frequency range and hence the larger your unconscious will become.

The NLP Communication Model describes how you create your reality from the stimulus you receive from your environment. All combined together—your body and its sensory equipment, your meta-programs, your current beliefs, your memories and ideas of past events, and the way you delete, distort, and generalise—results in the production of your conscious reality.

The way you talk to yourself is the single most important thing in your life

One of the many parts of your human experience is your internal voice. This is the voice with which you imagine and think. Your own awareness of your inner dialogue is unique to you and could be entirely unconscious—you may not be aware of it at all—or you could be somewhat conscious of it. The way you talk to yourself inside your own head is the single most important thing in your life.

Think about it.

Your inner dialogue may not only be your own voice, though. It can also include what you think others might say, for example your partner, parents, friends, colleagues, etc. Perhaps you think your boss will be angry at you and *you imagine the things she might have said or might say*. Perhaps you had an altercation with a stranger on your commute and the memory rings inside your head for the rest of the day and *you imagine the things she might have said or might say*. Even the voices that seem to belong to others all form part of your inner voice or inner dialogue. It also includes that secret voice you use to judge others. There's telling others what you think and then there is always that which you *really* think.

Perhaps you have multiple personalities in some way and a part of your mind seems to be someone else's voice. Voices like these inside your singular physical head also count as part of your own inner voice.

This internal dialogue that you narrate your life with, that you talk to yourself with, that congratulates you when things go good or attacks you when things go bad, with which you represent other significant people good or bad in your life, is important because the way you think leads to how you feel. How you feel in turn influences how you act. And how you act invites feedback from your environment.

The linguistic part of NLP is therefore about learning to notice and master your inner dialogue in order to create more desired results from the situations faced in life. If you are a thinking human being, then you most definitely have an inner voice.

Learn to take charge of your inner voice

To demonstrate the power your inner voice has over you think of a person you dislike somewhat. Imagine the words they say and the tone they use while talking. Think of their accent and notice the feelings they conjure up. Really hear their voice in your mind. Ask yourself where in your body you feel it.

What happens if you now change the tonal quality of the voice into that of Donald Duck? How does that change the quality of the feeling you now have? Is it still as painful as it was originally? Or is it now somewhat diminished? Is it even painful at all? Perhaps it's actually quite funny to you.

Now ask yourself where that feeling associated with this voice is located in your body. Really get a sense of it. Is it hot or is it cold? Does it pulse or move in some way? What speed is it going? Take the voice and feeling and move it to your big toe. How does that change the experience? Again, consider if it still has the same power over you or not. Has it become funnier or smaller perhaps? Does the voice now seem less important?

Congratulations. You have taken your first steps to mastering your inner voice. Such mastery is an important skill because your internal dialogue is the key to being able to change your inner world and thinking at your will.

The elephant and the rider

Your inner world is 90% unconscious. It is your unconscious thoughts that truly drive your actions in the real world. There is a growing body of scientific evidence that proves that when people are asked to explain why they took a particular action, their consciously derived logical reasoning happens after the event. This phenomenon is called *post hoc rationalisation.* This shows that your unconscious is actually in control of you. Your unconscious protects you and your internal reality and hence your unconscious governs your every action, whether you think you consciously took the action or not.

In his book, *The Happiness Hypothesis,* Jonathan Haidt describes the conscious mind as the rider of an elephant. The elephant represents the unconscious. It is the elephant that holds the true power to move the pair in any direction. The rider merely has a say. If the relationship between the rider and elephant is harmonious, the elephant will move in the direction the driver tells it to with full momentum, smoothly, and without hesitation. If the relationship is less than harmonious, the elephant may need more convincing to move or worse, it may decide to stay where it is or go in a different direction entirely. Just like your unconscious, the elephant is a beautiful, noble, powerful, loving creature, somewhat simplistic, childlike, and sensitive. It always takes the actions it judges to be best for its own self-preservation. Your elephant is governed by your inner world. And your inner world is represented by the thoughts and feelings you, the more intelligent conscious rider, feed to your elephant.

Figure 5 - Elephant and Rider

Your internal dialogue is key to the way you communicate with your inner elephant. Your elephant hears your every thought, whether it's your own voice or your internalised representations of other people's voices. Remember, the elephant is a sensitive, feeling being. When you dwell on what people will say or on painful situations in life, you will transfer that pain to your childlike unconscious self. Your elephant will then know where to move and with what energy, and you will take an action in the real world to attract the best matching outcome to that pain you were consciously dwelling on.

Now imagine that you were able to notice when your internal dialogue was somewhat negative and you were able to consciously alter it to see the love in the exchange. You were able to minimise the negativity in it or discard it entirely, and as a result, you were able to conjure up good feelings to feed to your elephant instead. As a result, your unconscious elephant now moves with this good energy and takes actions that attract a better outcome than in the previous example.

To minimise the negativity of your inner dialogue you need to become more skilful with the language with which you describe your inner world—your internal representation.

Increase your resolution on life

The resolution of your inner world is determined by the words you use, how you use them, and even how you say them. Angry shouting conveys a different meaning than a quiet loving whisper. Your vocabulary and your understanding of key language patterns are both important to how you analyse other people's language and how you communicate with your unconscious as well as others in your external environment. To understand these aspects of language is to have greater flexibility in how you are able to perceive your surroundings and also how you express your deepest thoughts. This flexibility of expressive, meaningful, emotionally rich description is essential for you to open up different opportunities for your life.

In our modern world, it is generally accepted that the standard colours we perceive include white, black, grey, brown, red, orange, yellow, green, blue, indigo, and violet. These words are the language we assign to the divisions in the colours we perceive through our sense of sight. It has been well documented that there are links between language and colour perception in different cultures. There are also different cultures with different languages that divide the visible light spectrum differently and other cultures that don't even have a word for colour. One example is the Himba tribe in Namibia who have no word for blue. Instead, blue is considered as a variant of green. Similarly, there are some shades of what we would consider to be green that the Himba consider separate colours entirely.

As individuals we perceive the world uniquely depending on the culture we were brought up in including our peer group, schooling, and of course, our families. Your life experience is unique to you, and you have as unique an education as any other person you have met. You have your own sense of the words you use to talk to yourself and to encode your experiences to memory. As covered previously, you form beliefs and automatic behaviours which enable you to keep up with the pace of life without having to consciously think through every last detail before taking action. Your beliefs form part of your unconscious system which is designed to look after you and what you think.

So far, we have considered the sense of sight. Now think about your sense of taste. Imagine you are in an Indian restaurant observing a young family eating their meal. The waiter serves them a curry rich in its combination of spices and flavours. What words would each character use to describe the dish? The children are young and find that the chilli heat is too overbearing for them and masks the true complexity of the flavour of the dish. Their parents, who are more seasoned curry veterans, are able to pick out the individual notes of the ingredients of the dish down to each spice and how they are balanced in the meal. As well as the flavour, they might also talk about texture and physical temperature and other more subtle qualities of the dish. They would also surely have a more nuanced opinion than their children would about improvements they might make to the curry or feedback for the chef.

The parents in this scenario are more flexible with their language and able to communicate about the curry in a more meaningful way than their children. Unlike their children who react to dismiss the food as too spicy, their parents are able to mindfully discern and appreciate the detail in the taste, discuss it, and offer creative ideas about it. Where in your life would it be useful for you to have this ability to stay in a conversation, appreciate the underlying message, and give a considered response, creating solutions instead of avoiding the situation? What other results could this bring for you? What options might open up?

There is a reason why education was historically the domain of the wealthiest and most privileged classes. It's no coincidence that the more you are able to study, the more specialised your language becomes and the more expert you become at any particular topic. Language is one the most important tools you need to create the results you want in life. Without the right language, you merely have a concept you are unable to communicate to others. Never stop educating yourself.

Your brain, neurology and your body

We have discussed the *Linguistic* and *Programming* aspects of NLP. N is for *Neuro*. The neural centre of your physical body is your brain. Your brain is also connected to the rest of your body via your central and peripheral nervous system which runs down through your spine and all the way out to your extremities. Your neurology is the equipment that receives input from your environment for your five main senses, and it also transmits signals to your muscles and physiology to drive the movement of your body including breathing, beating your heart, and digesting your food. As such, your neurology runs throughout your body.

This *Neuro* part of NLP concerns not only your brain's ability to learn but also the effect of your physiology on your mindset and how you think. Try the following experiment.

First, stand, shake your body out, and relax. Take stock of how you are feeling in this very moment. Do you generally feel happy and upbeat or somewhat down? Or perhaps you feel balanced and in not much of a strong mood either way

Now sit down. Screw your face up into a frown. Lean forward, tense your neck and your shoulders, and hunch over, fold your arms, and cross your legs. Speak the following statements out loud. As you say them, pay attention to which one feels more natural. Remember to hold your frown and crossed body language as you speak.

"I'm happy."

"I'm sad."

"I'm angry."

Now, stand and shake your body out again. Smile—really grin—and make a couple of star-jumps. Hold the pose as you land upright, erect and with arms outstretched and repeat the above statements again with this open body language. Notice how you really feel as you say them. You should find that it is difficult to be angry and down when your face is locked in a wide smile and your body is so open.

It is much easier to be happy when your body is positioned in one way and so much easier to be unhappy when it is positioned in another. This means that whenever you are in a low mood, you have an instant way to pick yourself up again if you want to. The *neuro* part of NLP is about your body and how you feel, both physically and emotionally, and how they relate to your thinking.

The ghost in the machine—your unconscious

As demonstrated earlier, you live mostly unconscious of what is happening in your body. You feel emotions in your thoughts but your body tends to only have a say when you experience pain. The common antidote to a physical pain or other symptoms is to suppress them with common supermarket drugs. But if your bodily processes are mostly unconscious, what if your symptoms are simply a physical expression of your unconscious? What if your symptoms are merely your body communicating with you about its particular needs? A simple example is if you don't eat for a while you develop stomach cramps, which is your body telling you to eat. If you become dehydrated, your throat, mouth, and tongue will dry up and feel uncomfortable, signalling you to drink some water. If you have an allergy and you are exposed to the allergen, your body will react, telling you to take action in some way to alleviate your symptoms.

Notice that the remedial action has now become a grey area involving a pharmaceutical rather than a natural food. With an allergy, you know to take some remedial action, probably an anti-histamine drug. In this grey area, you know you must take action, but the chances are the only options you know are to move away from the source of the allergen and take the drug. With thirst, you know to drink water. But with the allergen, it may be that you are not conscious yet of what foods or natural remedies your body is truly calling for. Of course there are extreme cases such as nut allergies where human-developed pharmaceuticals are an excellent choice for relief but in less serious cases, perhaps the body is calling for balance in some way?

With your stomach cramps, you know to eat food. At a higher level of consciousness, you might notice that you have a craving for a particular food. For example, although I was born and brought up in the UK, my family are of Bangladeshi origin. I have brown Asian skin and throughout my twenties and thirties, I constantly craved eggs. I could not get enough of them in my diet and two a day was sometimes not enough. The government advice at the time was to only eat three or four eggs per week or increase my risk of high cholesterol. But I couldn't help myself. I simply loved eggs.

I became worried enough about it when my friend discovered he had high cholesterol and so I went to my doctor for a check-up. Thankfully, there was no such issue for me. But I still craved eggs. One day, completely unrelated to this, my mother sat me down to discuss a symptom we both seemed to have with our feet. Her doctor had discovered that she was very low in vitamin D and after she had her boosters, her symptoms were gone, so she recommended me to check my vitamin D levels with my doctor. Lo and behold, I was also very low in vitamin D. As soon as I had my boosters, my foot cramps went away and so did my fifteen-year love affair for eggs. The change was literally overnight. They no longer had the same appeal.

Vitamin D is usually made by your skin when exposed to the sun. For people like me with darker skins, we don't have enough exposure to the sun in the UK climate and so we need to produce vitamin D from elsewhere and eggs are great sources for it. My body always knew at a level that I was not previously conscious of that I needed this vital building block in my diet. It communicated this need through a craving for this particular food which, to my conscious mind, merely seemed satisfying to ingest. Although I knew I had the craving I never previously understood why, so it was really an unconscious message from my gut to eat this food. This demonstrated for me the importance of listening to my body and being mindful of what I feed myself, whether that be food or physical exercise.

Your body is a physical expression of your state of being. How do you look? More importantly, how do you feel? Do you have niggling aches and pains that you put up with? Do you listen to your body? Do you move and stretch when you feel you need to? Similar to your body's gut cravings, pain also holds messages in your body. Stress tends to become locked up in your back and neck, close to your spine. At extremes, you might find you hold tension in your jaw as you grind your teeth. Are you aware of the tension in your body and the other energy currents and sensations you hold within? If you feel pain and tension, do you consciously think about whether it is from emotional stress and enquire into it or do you simply block it out with medications? If so what else are you blocking out in life?

We live in a culture where it is acceptable to take paracetamol, ibuprofen, aspirin, caffeine, etc. or prescribed drugs. Although modern medicine and pharmaceuticals certainly have a valid place, too often, we use them to mask the underlying issues rather than making adjustments to our lifestyle, because our current lifestyle is our comfort zone. How do you think this is relevant to you?

The modern condition

Your body evolved to cope with high stress for short periods of time to deal with immediate threats in your environment such as predators and other aggressors whom you would either fight or run away from. In any case, your internal systems were designed for *short stressful instances*, not *long stressful periods* of time. Nowadays, you face many demands with high workloads and the pressures of taking care of yourself and your family. Your body only knows how to treat this perpetual onslaught of one demand after another as constant threat. This is why you are stressed.

Under threat, your adrenaline and cortisol hormone

levels will fire up and your body will tense up, readying you to be able to instantly take the necessary physical action to survive. The cortisol will divert your resources to optimise your body's systems for quick fight or flight and supress your non-essential systems such as your immune system, digestive system, reproductive system, and growth processes. In the short term, if it means your survival, then this is of course a healthy response overall to immediate threats. The problem is that your stress is non-stop and so your body lives constantly in this heightened state. It is no coincidence that in the west generally, it is common for people develop diseases related to the non-essential systems cortisol will tend to suppress under immediate threat.

Of course the common solution is to consult a doctor who may prescribe drugs to alleviate these stress symptoms, but really, your body is calling you to move away from the source of your stress. Is this your job? Do you believe you rely on your job for your income? What does your income mean for your lifestyle? Review the previous chapters and notice how your beliefs affect your decisions in relation to your mind, body and diet. If you don't look after your mind-body, how can you effectively look after anything else in life?

Consider what the essential systems actually are for handling immediate danger. In high alertness, your conscious mind is fed threat assessment after threat assessment. How does that affect your RAS? How does that affect your point of view on life? Your body is kept in a certain state of tension in case you have to take quick physical action. How does that affect your body? Is it any wonder that modern people develop neurological conditions amongst others? Over a long enough period of time—say a career's worth of time—

will your neurological state perhaps permanently change as you develop the common mental disorders of old age like Alzheimer's Syndrome?

If you are like most people, you go about your life juggling a high-stress job and commute with family life, totally unconscious to the damage wrought on you by this modern lifestyle. As you experienced in the exercise earlier in the chapter, you can always choose to change your physiology to think positive thoughts whenever you want to. Many go to the gym or have fitness regimes and this regular physiology change does help, of course. But this fashion is only the perpetuation of the grand coping strategy of modern society. It's all simply a band-aid designed to keep you circulating money through society as you are sold on one fashionable trend after another, after another, after another, etc. The true problem is how disconnected you have become from your true animal nature and from the world around you. Think about it. When you were a hunter-gatherer, did you drink a high-caffeine, high-sugar energy drink first thing in the morning to keep you alert? Did you need an isolated protein recovery shake after hunting your prey or running away?

The real curse of modern life

The real curse of modern life is that you tend to live only aware of your outer experience of life. You go to work, pay bills, commute, pay rent, go shopping, go to events, do leisure activities, keep up appearances, and interact with others doing the same. It is very likely you don't take the time to meditate and really dedicate your attention to your internal experience—to really notice what is happening inside your body, to really understand your body's needs, and eat/exercise directed by feeling rather than fashion.

The real curse of modern life is that it you live constantly without looking beyond a basic "this feels good so I'll do this more," or "this feels bad so I'll react this way," without really knowing how good it will be for you in the long run. You might disagree, you might think you are responsible and you do consider your thoughts consciously, but again, have you ever questioned why you think the thoughts you do? If you have understood the content of this book this far, then you should be questioning your reality by now.

The real curse of modern life is that you spend your most important resource, your conscious uptime, on either firefighting your problems as they arise or engaging in addictive behaviours to take the pain away or distract you from your problems for a while. If you have a chronic condition, you probably spend a lot of time resenting how bad it is for you rather than considering what it is telling you and taking the correct actions to resolve it. I myself have a chronic skin condition that once became so bad it felt life threatening, but nowadays you wouldn't know it to look at me—you would think my skin looks perfect, but that's because I know how to manage my condition in a balanced way.

Worse still, others around you might give you their pity and so reinforce your reality, but it's never enough and secretly, you resent them for not suffering the same way you do. If you consult a doctor, you make them responsible for your recovery instead of taking that responsibility on yourself.

Basically, the real curse of modern life is that you have been taught to think that the way you live your life is normal. As a result, you wallow in your own self-pity and barely manage your external affairs while self-medicating away your spare time with drugs, food, sex, drink, computer games, social media, pop culture, etc.

It doesn't have to be like this.

A new beginning

If you are reading this book, then there is a part of you that knows there is more to life. And simply by reading it and being open to new concepts and ideas, you are already raising your consciousness to those previously unknown aspects of your life's hidden workings. All the answers lie within you. It's merely that you have spent your life looking to the outside instead. NLP offers you the tools to take charge of that overwhelming emotional stimulus from your outside experience and develop your conscious and unconscious thinking faculties to your best advantage. Later on, we will look at how you can then turn the volume up on your internally generated wisdom and truly live an inspired life.

This chapter has covered how your experience of life and your reality is constructed. With this very basic introduction to NLP, you now have an awareness of how you receive input from your environment and how you unconsciously filter it to suit what is easiest for you to put your conscious attention on. You now have an idea of how your belief system has been constructed and how it serves you best to look after your sense of self.

You now know enough to choose to question your beliefs if you want to. Are there some beliefs you have that once served to protect you but now seem to limit you, perhaps about your sense of worth, spiritually, or financially? What would you like to believe about yourself instead? Would you like to be a higher earner? Would you like to access passive income opportunities and really enjoy a healthy retirement in old age as a result? What opportunities could having different, more empowered beliefs open up for you? Well, you can have it if you choose to.

By now, you understand how important your internal dialogue is in attracting to you the results you want in life. If you are armed with the right beliefs expressed in the right language, this will automatically give you a more powerful mindset with which to really magnetise and take charge of your life. As mentioned previously, you don't know what you don't know.

Get a coach. Everyone who is the best in the world at what they do has a coach. Work with me or hire someone else, it doesn't matter. Choose someone who can really help you to shed light on your own inner self, your personal language patterns, and how you are currently constructing your reality. Find someone you actually resonate with who makes sense to you and whom you can hear, and remember to be coachable. No-one can change your reality for you because no-one can do your thinking for you. Take responsibility for your life starting right now!

CHAPTER 6

The Pain Of Disconnection

As you are now coming to see, you have lived for much of your life disconnected from your true spirit. You've been brought up to live in a world with a limiting belief that success is to have vast amounts of money and to spend it on lavish materialist lifestyle goodies. Fast fashion and retail therapy, the way the average consumer does them, are an addiction as much as any of the others previously listed because you get a dopamine boost each time you buy something nice. Little do you consider the harm done to others and the environment around you when you treat yourself.

Fast Fashion is an excellent documentary about retail fashion and films like *Supersize Me, An Inconvenient Truth,* and *Cowspiracy* are excellent starting points if you are interested in expanding your consciousness about how disconnected we have become in our modern consumerist world. How conscious or unconscious are you of these issues? Think about why you think the way you do about these issues. If your immediate feeling is to recoil from the idea of watching these titles, who has influenced your beliefs that led to these feelings in the first place? Do you notice your comfort zone at play in all this?

Back in the first chapter, you learnt to look at pain in terms of the traffic light colours of red, yellow, and green to judge your comfort level and to locate your place of healthy, growing pain. To quickly summarise again:

Green signifies the comfort zone, a place where the status quo is maintained and life is at least predictable, even if you are not entirely satisfied with it. It is a real challenge to move out of green because although life might be rather dull and uninspiring, at least you know what to expect.

Red is the danger zone, the total opposite of green, where you are frozen in fear and unable to do anything consciously or take a truly considered action. This is where you live life firefighting, in constant panic and in constant reaction to your circumstances. Like green, red is not a place where you can grow easily.

Yellow is a healthy stretch away from green, which is still in sight, but is the space you can expand into safely. If green is your comfort zone, then yellow is where you are outside your comfort zone, a little uncomfortable but able to grow. In this space, you face challenge but unlike red, you are able to pause, slow your thoughts down, and truly consider your actions. In yellow, you exercise courage and faith.

When you jump into the unknown, it's uncomfortable simply because it's unfamiliar and you're not used to it. However, transformation into something new can only exist outside of what you know. So in order to grow, you have to explore beyond your comfort zone, which therefore requires you to face some of the pain hiding in your psyche of which you are most likely unconscious, to take responsibility for it, and let it go. The previous chapter described the toolkit that is NLP which can help you to uncover and heal some of this pain and thereby attract better results into your life.

The Universal Challenge

At first, it seems difficult to do new actions. Perhaps you have to rethink some relationships or your friends might find it hard to see you in a different way to how they currently see you, but this is, in fact, the Universal Challenge. This is about how much you want to achieve your transformational goal. Remember, you have always created your own results in life. You have played a certain part and attracted a certain set of people around you. These people have their own individual unique beliefs about you which have resulted in the masks you and everyone else now project to each other. Each person now plays a certain role in your social circle. It's a tight-knit web and seemingly difficult to change. But you aren't entirely happy with the part you play.

It's especially tight where your family is concerned. Perhaps you have over-protective parents. It could be that they love you and have always wanted the best for you but at the same time, you might find their love restrictive and stifling. Perhaps you secretly resent them but you politely accept their offerings and advice because it's easier to do so than to upset them. You don your mask to protect them from what you truly think and you disconnect from your own true heartfelt desire. In this way, you sacrifice your own true desire in order to serve your parent's desires instead and you put a brave face on it. It pains you somewhat but it's simply easier. This is a green comfort zone type of pain. The pain communicates that you want something different but it's less painful to stick with the current situation rather than to follow the path of your heart. Does this feel familiar to you?

You might feel similarly about your job. You might feel stuck in a rut, merely happy that you have the means to maintain your lifestyle and family. You might wish for a promotion but really, you know somewhere deep inside that those opportunities are for someone else. Your managers don't regard you that way, or the jobs on offer aren't quite the right fit for you, or you're not young enough, you're the wrong gender, you don't want to do the required study, etc. Or maybe you only want a pay-rise. You've been there long enough and developed a real expertise for how you do your job and you deserve to be recognised. Or perhaps it's simply that your pay hasn't gone up as much as inflation has and the money you make just doesn't buy you as much as it once did.

These are all simply excuses—your own limiting beliefs that preserve your current reality. You put up with it but you secretly resent it. You might act up a little here or there, but not enough to get you fired and you definitely won't actually quit. You might look at LinkedIn to see what's on offer elsewhere but you won't actually apply for anything else. By now, you're at the top of your grade anyway and you wouldn't get that money elsewhere. You have to think about your family and what about the new commute, could you get the same pay elsewhere, etc.

This is simply the Universe showing up to protect your

reality. These thoughts are your unconscious beliefs about your current situation—your environment, family, friends, colleagues, and other actors who tie you into your current life show up and keep you stuck. All these limiting beliefs draw the boundaries of your green comfort zone. You might test these boundaries, pass through into yellow, and try new things, but you don't remain in yellow for long enough for it to become habit. Another limiting belief you might have is that "old habits die hard."

As you understand by now, you create your own reality from the input you receive through your senses and how your brain processes these signals. Review the previous chapter on NLP if you need to. Now, if you create your reality, you also create the problems you see before you. Every event in life is merely a challenge of creative problem solving through which you develop life skills. You have been designed to simply flow from one event to the next in life. When things stop flowing and you are stuck, it causes frustration. You don't want to stay where you are but it seems too difficult to move forward.

Remember that optimism, creativity, and relentless drive you once had as a child? Well that is simply no longer there. Your lifetime of education, career, and all-consuming media and current affairs has put paid to that. Your creative muscle has become so weak, it now hurts to even consider the solution. But you need a strong creative muscle in order to really take charge of your Universe and your reality.

If you feel trapped in life, no matter what the situation, then you face an opportunity to grow and to develop your creative ability to find the solution, and when you overcome the challenge, that skill will become a new resource for you for the rest of your life. It might not seem possible right now, so suspend your belief for a moment and ask yourself how amazing your life would be if you could feel like a child again—optimistic, open, and unstoppable in your pursuit of simply having fun and growing. How would it feel to live those qualities again in the now as your adult self?

Feel good and notice your balance

We already established in the previous chapter that changing your body language can really raise your mood. It is actually impossible to be down and depressed while jumping for joy and screaming, "*Yes, yes, yes!*" If you have ever regularly done any form of cardiovascular exercise, you will know the effect getting air into your lungs and using your body has on your mood. It feels so good because you were designed by nature to run and hunt and survive. This is a far cry from the modern sedentary corporate lifestyle you've been taught to take up in your life.

Ever since the dawn of humanity, our ancestors had to compete for food and sex in order to pass their genes on to future generations. This evolutionary programming to procreate and further our species lies so deep within, it drives every aspect of our existence even in the modern world. It's why you earn money. It's why you set up home. It's why you dress to impress. It's why you want to succeed in life in order to attract the best partner to have the best children with and through them, you pass on your genes and knowledge for the benefit of future generations.

Within your brain lies a reward circuit which evolved to

incentivise you to take actions that secure the survival of your genes. When you exercise and when you eat, it's this structure that makes you feel really good. This is a result of a flood of dopamine released to signal that you took a relevant action towards your procreation which you feel as a pleasurable high. At its most natural extreme it's that sense of ecstasy you get from sexual release which is in itself the reward for passing on your genes. The closer any activity you do is to this primary genetic goal, then the greater the rush and the more powerful the high. This explains then why eating nourishing food doesn't deliver quite the same pleasure as pure emotionally connected, love-based sex. This reward circuit is *the* primary driver in your life. And whether you know it or not, you have borne all the pain of your modern life in the hope of passing on your genetic wisdom. Notice how even from a genetic level, a successfully directed life is supposed to *feel* good.

But in modern life, not everything that feels good is necessarily actually good for you. This is because many organisations have developed products specifically designed to hijack your reward circuit, to create within you an addiction for their product. Big business requires mass consumers who are hungry for their products and they invest big money to keep your consumership. And they are so devious, you think you choose to consume their products out of your own free will without their influence.

Left alone, your brain exists in natural healthy balance. Our consumerist society is designed to upset your balance in perpetuity—by artificially raising your dopamine so unnaturally high to levels where your brain recalibrates its sense of "normal." This, in turn, sets your sense of "normal" unnaturally high and you now need that addictive substance or behaviour to feel normal, rather than that comparatively boring food or sex you used to crave. You have become addicted.

Think about a seemingly innocent caffeine hit from a high-sugar energy drink. Both the sugar and the caffeine feel so good and temporarily spike your dopamine to an *abnormally* high state. Time passes and your dopamine levels drop back to normal and you feel comparatively worse but generally okay. As you consume more of the drink, you still feel the rush but you find the high doesn't last as long, nor is it as powerful. This is where your dopamine system is beginning to adapt to this new abnormal high. That point where you feel like crap until you get that energy drink into your system—that is the point of recalibration. What you once considered "normal" now feels low compared to the artificial high you now need to feel balanced, i.e. you have developed a dependency on that energy drink to make you feel normal. Now, in order to feel the high again, you have to up your intake of the drink. This chasing effect is the escalation of your addiction and so becomes your downward spiral away from natural normal healthy balance. The energy drink feels good physically but this feeling is artificial.

But although the drink makes you high, the high sugar content eats away at your body. As well as feeling good in your brain for a powerful short-term, your body presents other less intense signals to warn you that something is not right. At first, these signals are very subtle, especially compared to those relentless monster-sized cravings for that drink, and you dismiss them until one day, your doctor diagnoses you with early onset diabetes. Your unbalanced system is now in catastrophic decline.

Think about what products you use and behaviours you employ and notice whether they seem in balance to you or not. Are some of them crutches? Go back to whom you were five or ten years ago and compare. What do you notice? Are there some differences you believe to be age related or genetic? Are they really or are these more limiting beliefs you have about yourself? Finally, think of someone your age now whom you would consider to be in balance. How good would it feel to have this balance for yourself?

Your neurology and alignment

It is estimated that your brain has over eighty billion neurons and it is widely accepted that this is the seat of your logical mind. We also know that your gut lining contains approximately one hundred million neurons and from the energy drink example above, you can see how this can affect your behaviour.

In that example, we covered dopamine which is the hormone that governs your sense of motivation. Another important hormone is serotonin, which your body uses to signal general satisfaction for food, sex, sleep, happiness, etc. When you feel well, the chances are that your serotonin levels are high. When you feel low, it is likely your serotonin levels are also low. In this way, your gut influences what foods you crave. If you have ever had a "gut feeling," you know it can also influence your decision making. If your gut is satisfied, you will produce serotonin and you will feel satisfied. To continue the energy drink example above, on a physical level, you might feel good drinking it because of the high dopamine, but it might not raise your serotonin so much. This will cause you to feel good in the short-term but somehow unsatisfied.

Your heart contains around forty thousand neurons. This may seem small compared to the brain and gut but it is still a large number to be concentrated around one particular organ in your body. The chances are you *know* when something feels really good in your heart and how that affects the rest of your system. Think about when you last fell in love. You had butterflies in your stomach and all logic went out of the window as you took one risky action after another after another to be closer to your muse.

At the other extreme, if you have ever experienced true grief then you know, from the process of letting go, the emotional power all those tender memories of your loved one conjure up. You cycle through memory after memory as you share with your friends and family—the good times, the sad times, the happy times, the melancholy times, the angry times, etc. You experience a powerful emotional rollercoaster of ecstasy and sorrow that eventually leaves you drained of tears and all emotion by the end of the process. These powerful feelings come from inside your spirit and through your heart. People might refer to this feeling as heartbroken.

Remember, you're mostly unconscious and this part of yourself that holds these feelings runs deep inside you. After a lifetime of studies and career efforts, your life is now an established routine that takes place mostly in the physical world. But at what point did you change from a child free to play with joyful creative abandon to an adult with bills and a job on the uninspiring treadmill of life? You may still have moments where your heart wakes up and you feel the ecstasy of a brilliant idea that totally captures your imagination. But now, as quickly as it is born, you quickly crush it and bury it under the logic of your head. You tell yourself you can't follow your heart's direction because this will be difficult, or that will be hard, or how will you pay for it, or what will your friends/partner/parents/people think? You feel your heart light up with passion and then your head takes over with rational logistics, and so your idea dies. Your heart points out one direction and your head takes another. It wasn't always this way. If you are especially unlucky, you might not even be able to feel your heart anymore because it has become so quiet and almost switched off in comparison.

When you were born, you had no sense of logic at all. You were purely heart led. You were an entirely feeling being. As your parents and loved ones nurtured you and brought you up, you learnt to behave in certain ways which they taught you were good and to stop doing the things they taught you were bad. You learnt to walk, talk, read, and write, to sleep at certain times and eat and play at others. Also, you were given certain toys to play with depending on your sex and slowly, society began to shape you.

After a few years, you went to nursery and socialised with other toddlers. You learnt to play nicely with other children and the social rules of sharing with others and treating them with respect. As you grew older, you learnt arithmetic and art, science and languages, humanities, etc. Eventually, you went to high school and then university until you entered the workforce and the rest is history. You learnt to think logically with your head and were prepared to take up your position as a useful member of society. You practiced with your head so much that this part of you was so loud compared with the sotto voce of your heart.

As a baby, you were an entirely creative being living in a world of infinite imagination. You could fantasise anything, and there were no limits to your ideas and inspirations. Your life was led purely by your heart. As you grew up, you were taught to develop your logical senses. You were so in tune with the infinite energy of youth that if you asked too many questions, the comparatively lethargic adults around you would get irritated and dismissive of you and slowly, you learned to be less creatively minded and more logically minded. Yet the closest you have ever been to a truly creative imaginative genius is when you were an infant when you were led purely by your heart. Now, with the voice of reason so loud compared to the voice of your heart, the trick is to revisit your thinking and learn to quieten your mind.

The modern education system drilled out of you that there are other sources for ideas other than simply your head. You are more a heart-led feeling being than a head-led logical being, yet society encourages you to mask your true feelings and to live from your head instead. As you reach middle age, you notice how much less fun life is now that you've entered the rat race and you look ahead to your retirement with a feeling of resentment that the rest of your life is downhill from now. It gets you down and before long, you start living for your Friday night and the weekend when you can escape temporarily. Or maybe you switch off even during the week with whatever harmless escapist hobbies you have—maybe gaming or television or the news or social media, etc?

Your head says you're doing the right thing because you have to do something to pay the bills or how would you survive? But your heart isn't in your work. Your situation is uncomfortable because your heart and mind are not aligned. It pains your very spirit. And left long enough, your survival instinct will kick in. You'll have what most people will dismiss as a mid-life crisis.

All is not as it seems

As a human being, you exist in many dimensions. The spatial dimensions of forward/backward, left/right, and up/down are easy to understand. However, time is different. It cannot be viewed simply by turning your head to face in a particular direction. If the spatial dimensions allow you to locate yourself physically, then time allows you to track movement between locations from one moment to the next. Your experience of time is that it only flows in one direction from past to present. Whereas you can easily move yourself within the three spatial dimensions through time, you cannot simply move yourself to twelve hours into the future without waiting for twelve hours to elapse first. Nor can you remain still at any single point in time like you can remain still within the spatial dimensions. This is because time is your experience of the flow of present moment to present moment and this flow never stops.

You have memories of past events which you can revisit in your mind and then predict what might happen in future if you take certain actions. A large part of your personal identity is made up of what you remember of events from your past. From the last chapter on NLP, you have already seen that everything you recall from the past is never the whole truth and only a filtered part of the event that happened. What you remember is always merely a partial recording of the whole scene. This is because your ability to recall is a conscious process that picks the parts of your memory relevant to the outcome you wish to confirm at the time of recall.

Your memory is actually perfect as recorded by your unconscious. Remember, there is much more information that comes in through your senses than you could ever consciously handle. Much, therefore, remains unavailable to your conscious mind until it becomes relevant, if ever. Your unconscious constantly protects your sense of self and as a result, it only presents new facets of past memories to your conscious mind when it thinks you now have the resources to consciously handle them. In this way, your mind has a clever way to protect you from having to consciously deal with particularly traumatic experiences. Your ability to consciously recall never reveals the full story of the event that happened at the time. This means that the past as you think it happened is never the entire truth. The past as you consciously know it is therefore an illusion that doesn't exist. This, of course, informs the actions you take in the present.

Think about how you recall the past. Do you generally remember the bad things that don't feel good, or do you only remember the good in things? What is your perspective and what opportunities are you open to seeing?

The Karpman Drama Triangle

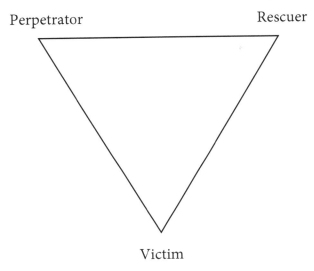

Perpetrator   Rescuer

Victim

Figure 6 - Karpman Drama Triangle

In previous chapters, we have viewed life mainly from the perspective of being a victim of modern society. In 1968, Stephen Karpman published an article outlining his theory of the archetypes someone seeing the world from this perspective might observe. The Karpman Drama Triangle is made up of three archetypes: the Victim, the Perpetrator, and the Rescuer. When you view life through this lens, others in your life will tend to show up as one of these three types. If you are like most people, you find it easy to see yourself as the Victim in some way based on what you recall about the past.

Back in 2013, at my lowest point, I felt like I was a victim of everything in life. At this time, I genuinely did not believe that

I had ever pursued any real direction of my own. Instead, my parents, friends, teachers, or bosses told me what to do and where to go next. For me, it was merely easier and involved less pain to mask my true emotions and simply follow their wishes. If any of my friends from this period ever read this, please, know that I am eternally grateful for your influence on me in my character-building years. The fun we shared was genuine. I simply had considerable secret stuff going on behind my mask.

I mainly saw my life as a consequence of other people directing me. I had always been weak-willed and I generally went through life looking for other people to learn from and to lead me. Beyond my parents, it would be my friends or my colleagues, etc. This low sense of self was reflected in my skin throughout my life. I had eczema and psoriasis from my earliest childhood and as a result, I was a constantly scratching, uncomfortable, itchy mess. In my pre-teens, people said hurtful things about it and I went through my twenties feeling extremely unattractive, even though I received a lot of attention from women. I had many "I don't deserve..." and "I'm not worthy of..." style limiting beliefs that stopped me from pursuing many relationships I could have had.

My career started in 2000 as a result of my first temp agency role after university. Generally, I worked in the UK public sector and I faced redundancy twice in my corporate career. Either I quit or I was absorbed into different organisations and as a result, it never felt like I spent enough time in the same place to become known well enough to be considered for promotion. A public sector salary is not much compared to the private sector anyway so I was always broke, and although I developed highly specialised skills, I remained below management grades my entire career.

At age thirty-six, I lagged far behind my friends who were now settled down, married, and having kids. I was still single, super socially awkward, and tragically unable to woo women even when they displayed extremely strong signals of attraction towards me. My career was going nowhere and I was up to my eyes in debt. I was in a really sorry state and I hated myself thoroughly. If I hadn't been so weak willed and powerless to control myself, rather than not caring when crossing busy London roads, I might have simply ended it and put myself out of my own misery.

Although this story was my truth then, it is not my truth now. I will discuss the nature of "truth" and how we perceive "reality" in the next chapter, but suffice it to say as well as the scarcity evident in the above account, you will notice how inward-looking and self-centred my perspective was. This is an example of viewing life through the lens of a Victim.

In simple terms, the Victim in any given situation is the person being harmed. Usually, the person doing the harm is seen as the Perpetrator and the person helping is the Rescuer. I say "usually" because sometimes, the Rescuer might do more harm than good and the Perpetrator might exercise tough love. These descriptions are transactional, meaning the different actors in the scenario can switch roles. Also note that these archetypes are not limited to actual people but can be specific situations, organisations, or objects, e.g. red bills threatening to cut you off, bailiff notifications, etc.

In my situation described above, I was very much the Victim of other people. No one was actually sent to harm me. It was merely that my outlook on life was such that

I perceived people as either harming me *intentionally* as Perpetrators or *unintentionally* as Rescuers.

Perpetrators are not necessarily bullies, per se. They could be acting out of love. It's more that they represent people, organisations, or situations that feel demeaning to the Victim. For instance, I felt overworked in my job. In this case, my bosses and my workload fit the Perpetrator archetype. Generally, my bosses were good people and I got on with them very well on a personal level, but this was my Victim point of view of my situation.

Even the best-intentioned Rescuers can sometimes do more harm than good and appear as Perpetrators instead. For example, my amazing dad has come to my rescue a million times in my life for which I am hugely grateful. I am so fortunate to have had a dad full of such unconditional love. But in my victimhood, I mostly received his help as a force that stifled my growth prematurely, rather than letting me grow through making my own mistakes. As a result, I simply developed a dependence on him to rescue me when times were tough and he learnt to depend on me needing to be rescued by him.

It's important to note that if you play the Victim in a situation, you automatically place others in the role of Perpetrator or Rescuer. Remember, everyone at any one time is a combination of this triad. My bosses made genuine work requests of me. They were hired to do their job the same way I was hired to do mine, and in this case, their job required them to ask me to do mine. By receiving their professional requests like a Victim, I acted like a Victim. This simply made me difficult to work with and therefore to them, perhaps, like a Perpetrator.

Similarly, if you show up as Rescuer to someone who is not looking for help, you will automatically be placing them in the role of the Victim. Again, no one likes to feel victimised, so the Rescuer can be seen as the Perpetrator. I used to work way beyond the required hours. There was once a Friday night when everyone had left the office to enjoy the weekend and unbeknownst to anyone, I stayed at my desk until 1:30 a.m. I was at the end of a six-month project I was about to roll out the following Monday. My inner Rescuer felt I had to stay behind to fix the bugs before I could leave. Personally, I felt I deserved congratulations and recognition for this unnecessary display of dedication. But the truth is, absolutely nobody asked me to stay behind. That I felt I had to take this action simply made my managers feel bad. And of course, had anyone known, they would definitely have ordered me to go home and told me to not worry about it and to enjoy my weekend. In this case, my inner Rescuer was received as a Perpetrator.

As you can see, the Drama Triangle is a complex dynamic with many pitfalls that can lead you into messy situations. If you come at life as a Victim in some way, you are most likely victimising others also simply by seeing life from this perspective.

You will also tend to look to your past to confirm your low view of life in the present, which will influence the situations you invite into your life in your future. As a Victim, you'll see few realistic choices, if any, and this will make you anxious. As well as being depressed about the past, you are now also anxious about the future too. The future hasn't even happened yet and you worry about it and spend your energy to find strategies to mitigate every circumstance you can imagine. You stress yourself out by applying your conscious thought to cycle back to the past, feel down about it, wish it was different, and calculate what's going to happen next. Victim thinking places your mind on anything but events happening right here, right now, in this present moment.

Remember, your conscious mind can only handle 7 ± 2 things in any given instant. What thoughts are you filling your conscious capacity with? If you're constantly living in the past and projecting into a future that hasn't happened yet, what are you missing in the present right here and right now? If this does sound like you, then is your current thinking really serving you?

The Empowerment Dynamic

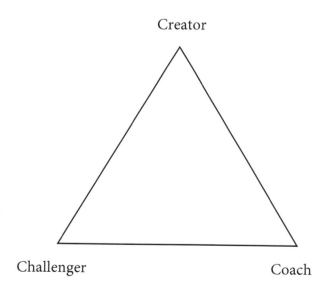

Figure 6 - The Empowerment Dynamic

One solution to the Karpman Drama Triangle is The Empowerment Dynamic which was created by David Emerald. From this perspective, instead of seeing things as a Victim, you *take responsibility* for your own thinking and assume the role of the Creator. In this framework, rather than seeing Perpetrators and Rescuers in your environment, you see these people as Challengers and Coaches.

The Creator takes responsibility for his thinking and is thus present in the moment. He formulates his actions and navigates to a more desirable future. When someone comes along and presents a seeming problem, the Creator sees a challenge that can be overcome. Simply by knowing from the outset the problem has at least one solution, he has already set his mind to looking for them. He has a more abundant attitude and can break down even the largest, most complex problems into manageable chunks with ease and staying in the moment, he focuses on the next step most likely to lead to a desirable solution. The Creator is forgiving of others he interacts with who help him to shape his future. Either they are Challengers who help to test his design for life or they are Coaches who show up to help. He is full of gratitude for his life—past, present, and future—and for all the people that show up in it.

For example, recently I was stopped for speeding on the motorway. The speed I was driving was enough that the police officer who stopped me had the power to instantly ban me if he wanted to. I love driving and I count myself extremely fortunate to have come away from this interaction still legally able to drive. I don't write this to brag, simply to demonstrate the power of the Creator mindset.

It was one a.m. on a weekday and I travelled on a free-flowing four-lane motorway in the fast lane. All other traffic—and there wasn't much—occupied the first two lanes only. I really do savour the experience of driving as it is a flow experience for me. Speed is a way to keep me conscious in the moment. On this particular journey, I cruised in my usual relaxed manner. I do not race others, change lanes needlessly, tailgate, or take part in any other form of aggressive driving. Especially on motorways, I like to drive efficiently and leave plenty of space for others to join traffic or overtake, etc. and the whole thing is usually a calm, seamless experience for me, just at high speed. I was cruising along listening to an audiobook when I saw blue lights in my rear view mirror.

Of course, my first thought was shock, surprise, and horror. I knew the speed I was doing and I knew the consequences if I were to be stopped, and there I was—being stopped. Quite rightly, I was scared and in fear. Of course, I pulled over, stopped my engine, and opened the window. I knew my speed, I knew the consequences, and I knew my actions leading up to the moment I saw the blue lights. I also knew that I am not a dangerous driver and drive at high speed precisely to feel more awake which seems safer all around to me. But I also knew the law. I knew that I was very clearly on the wrong side of it, and the police officer absolutely had the right to ban me. I had zero control in the situation so I simply accepted that whatever was about to happen was about to happen. In my Creator mindset, I was simply in the moment, calm and open to any result. Notice my detachment here, or leaving space for the abundance of possibility in my frame as a Creator.

A previous Victim conscious version of me would have panicked and frozen in fear for a while, knowing that I was about to lose my right to drive and with that, my freedom to move around my rural neighbourhood easily and conveniently. I would have been scared and I would have stayed in that mode while talking to the police officer. Possibly, I would probably have reacted and made arguments to defend myself in an obnoxious way. I might even have lied about my instruments being wrong or some other unwise course of action. Worse, I could have raised my voice and called the officer names or employed other unhelpful strategies to inflict some pain on the man whom I "knew" was about to take away this source of so much bliss in my life, my right to drive. This Victim version of me would be focused on a future in which I would be banned from driving and full of anxiety as a result. I would have perceived the police officer mainly as someone about to Perpetrate a harm on me in the name of Rescuing me and other drivers from my actions. Notice the stark contrast between my old scarcity conscious Victim mentality and my now abundance conscious Creator mindset.

So what actually what happened?

After what felt like a long wait, the police officer crouched beside my window. He was silent and definitely seething but he did an admirable job of retaining his composure. I took responsibility and opened the conversation in a calm, respectful way. He matched my tone and followed my lead. He asked if I knew why he stopped me and if I knew what speed I was travelling at. I answered truthfully and everything I gave the officer communicated that I was conscious, clear thinking, calm, respectful, and attentive to him and responsible for myself.

The officer gave me his observation of the event and acknowledged that although I was speeding, he didn't necessarily consider my driving dangerous, per se. At such speed, he had to wonder if I would even stop for him. He had pulled me over because he had to make an example for the other road users. Fair enough. He told me that earlier that evening, he had witnessed a fatality on the road. I felt his pain. He gave me every chance to explain my reason for driving at such a pace. Was I hurrying to my child's birth or a loved one's deathbed? Was there an emergency of some sort?

There wasn't, and I knew this was not the right time to present my own opinion about speed and safety. I merely spoke calmly when I was spoken to and answered his questions simply, clearly, and politely. He checked that I was aware that he could give me an instant driving ban and the impact that would have on my personal and professional life. I lived in a rural area at the time and I knew such a ban would be massively inconvenient for me. Nevertheless, I accepted that the application of the law was entirely in the police officer's control and every single answer I had for him was a thought I consciously vetted before I formed the words and spoke.

The police officer's anger was quelled and he stated he would let me continue my journey without punishing me. I communicated my abundant thanks and my respect for his authority. I really would have calmly taken the ban if he had decided it to apply it. I expressed my respect for his experience of the death he had witnessed earlier that day. Throughout the conversation, I connected with him on a human level, respecting his authority and his feelings.

Whether you approve of my speeding or not, I am sure you will agree that I had a tremendously lucky outcome. My part was clean of any Victim behaviour and as purely of the Creator archetype as I could muster. This Challenge had only shown up because I had Created it. I was, after all, responsible for speeding so I had to accept my fate. I received the wisdom of the police officer as lessons from someone Coaching me to be better, rather than as someone Perpetrating on me or unwantedly Rescuing me.

Making the shift

As the Creator of your life and your current circumstances, you always have the choice to learn from your past experiences rather than dwelling on how depressed they make you feel. To make the shift, you have to be able to separate your feelings from the events in the past and view the event from outside without emotion. This requires you to take responsibility for your results in life so far. This might be a big challenge, especially if you are recovering from a massive trauma. But once you are able to accept responsibility, the real work can begin. By learning to forgive the other actors in the situation and letting go of your emotional ties to them and the event itself, you can begin the process of quieting your mind and moving on. Only with a quiet mind will you be able to appreciate your life experience as your gift and understand that the challenges you have faced actually contain wisdom designed specifically for you. And such wisdom is a unique gift designed especially for you, as long as you are willing to see it this way.

By letting go of these feelings and emotions, you will learn to truly to love yourself. In your victimhood, when you cycled through and relived your bad experiences over and over again, you harmed yourself more than helping. By engaging the sympathy of your loved ones and friends, you simply recruited others to give you love from the outside. Unfortunately, this also had the effect of stamping an impression of your identity in their minds which, of course, makes them resist your transformation into your Creator. But transform you must and if you are able to, you will now use your mental faculty to go into the past to learn lessons from it rather than be depressed by it.

As a Creator learning from past events, you will no longer be pained when imagining a future that fills you with anxiety. By learning these lessons, you will now see new options. These were always there but you were either not able to see them before or not strong enough to take them then. Your logical mind will step in and tell you how impractical and unlikely these new options are for you, but they will fill your heart with joy and excitement, nevertheless. Yes, these are heartfelt feelings. When you get to this point, you know that your spirit is calling. And now that you have some mastery over your thinking, thanks to tools like NLP or meditation, you will be able take charge of your logical mind and set to work planning for your success instead of spending your time anticipating your failure.

As the Creator of your life, you now have control over your past and your future, and your life is filled with an abundance of strength and positivity in anticipation of that. Every experience in your life becomes wonderful and precious as you simply flow from moment to moment in true connection with your environment around you.

Ask yourself where in your past you showed up as the Victim. Were you genuinely powerless in the situation or was it simply a Challenge you weren't equipped for at the time? How about now? Can you identify all the Victim, Perpetrator, and Rescuer nodes in the Victim Triangle and how they played out? How does it feel to notice which parts of the event were your own doing? What could you have done differently that might have led to a better result? When you think about that now, how does it feel?

CHAPTER 7

The Three Principles

In 1973, Sydney Banks, a ninth-grade educated welder, experienced a profound spiritual insight into the nature of human existence. In a conversation with a marriage counsellor he had met at a conference, Syd described in lengthy detail how he was an insecure mess, to which the therapist replied, "I've never heard such nonsense in my life." Syd heard something in this response that was quite different to the words spoken by the therapist. In his own words:

> "What I heard was: there's no such thing as insecurity, it's only Thought. All my insecurity was only my own thoughts! It was like a bomb going off in my head… It was so enlightening! It was unbelievable… [And after that,] there was such beauty coming into my life."

The *words* spoken by the therapist and the *meaning* Syd took from them are separate entities, and this led Syd to conclude there are three foundational principles that create and govern the entirety of the human experience of life: Universal Mind, Universal Consciousness, and Universal Thought.

From his humble beginnings, Syd became a prolific author and a world-renowned teacher to innovators in psychology and psychiatry amongst others. After his insight, Syd dedicated the rest of his life to alleviating human suffering through teaching people to access their innate mental health through the Three Principles.

The Great Illusion

Throughout this book, you have come to learn that your thinking is fallible. This is because your beliefs are fallible. This, in turn, is because the information that flows in through your senses is filtered through your unconscious mind. You now understand that only a fraction of that information is presented to your conscious mind. In your previous thinking, you were always driven by scarcity and victim-minded thinking. In those times where you previously felt bad in life, you simply accepted this state to be the truth and reacted accordingly without knowing you could quite easily choose to feel good instead.

Through these pages, you have been introduced to strategies to question your thinking and your belief systems, to give you power over your consciousness, and rein in that unconscious elephant-like being inside of you. You have learnt some strategies to quieten your mind of these negative thoughts and feelings. Without these distractions, you will now be able to hear your heart's desire. This is the calling of your soul and when you feel it, you will find it is confirmed by how good you feel right to the core of your being.

The Three Principles of Sydney Banks' insight are the same wisdom as that of Plato in his Allegory of the Cave. In Plato's version, he described prisoners in a cave only able to see the shadows of reality cast on the wall. The shadows are the only forms the prisoners know which for them, are their reality. But you and I know that those shadows are cast by objects held in front of a light. We know that there is indeed something that lies behind their form.

Words are of the form. Ideas are of the formless.

Look beyond the words. The words are like the shadows. There is always an underlying concept beneath the words. Listen for the meaning beyond the words. You already know that your memories of the past are actually illusions that don't exist except inside your own head. Your past is an illusion of your ego. Inside your head, your ideas take the form of a conceptual understanding of which your inner dialogue only forms a part. Your conceptual understanding of anything is more than simply the words you pick to describe it but also inner versions of your main senses. You imagine how things look, sound, feel, taste, and smell. When you wish to communicate these concepts to others, you have to use words and gestures and sometimes, other creative methods like pictures or poetry. In the physical realm, you communicate ideas by giving your internal concepts physical form. This is the act of *creation*. Inside your head, your internal concepts take a mental form. Everything you think is simply a thought projection of ideas. So where do your original ideas actually come from?

Mind, Consciousness and Thought

To live as a creator is to live with your mind so quiet of negative thoughts that you are able to hear your heart's inspiration. When your mind is empty, nature automatically fills it and new thoughts present themselves. Your empty mind, in this case, is your *personal mind,* and the new thoughts that present themselves seem to land in your heart. Your personal mind is like a canvas upon which you paint your *personal thoughts,* negative or positive. In this book, you have learnt by now that you can always take responsibility for your personal thoughts if you really want to. This means using your will to take charge of your *personal consciousness.* And it is with your consciousness that you see what you see of your reality, i.e. your creation.

In that silence of your mind, you receive inspiration in the form of *insights*—or sights from within. These have a very different quality to your usual recycled ideas that you process with your *personal thought.* These insights feel brand new, like revelations, and you feel as excited as you did when you were an optimistic toddler all those years ago before life got the better of you and you became jaded by years of practical routine and soul-destroying stress. These insights are of *original thought* or *Universal Thought.* As the name implies, Universal Thought belongs to the Universe.

Universal Thought resonates with your heart and you can only become conscious of it when your mind is free from your usual thinking. You feel Universal Thought flowing through you as big, exciting original ideas, but this knowledge doesn't belong to you any more than it belongs to anyone else. These insights also land in others who are similarly magnetised to attract them also. And you may find that you attract more of such people around you as you yourself become a more abundant creative thinker. Your insights are revelatory gifts whose intentions are to be born through you into the physical realm where they can benefit others. If you block the flow, then the insight is born through someone else instead. This is like different groups of scientists making the same discoveries independently of each other and racing to be the first to publish their findings.

Universal Thoughts come from outside of you from something that is far greater than you or any other single human mind. They come from the *Universal Mind*. This is the great divine spiritual energy of the Universe of which we are all an individual expression. Just like the Universe is fractal in the physical plane, so it is also fractal on the spiritual plane. This "original" thought is always there in every single moment of your life. The reason you cannot always receive it is because the human condition is to live life concerned with the needs of the ego rather than the soul. Original thought permeates the Universe like the Cosmic Microwave Background Radiation observed by astronomers—an almost undetectable remnant from The Big Bang—and like the CMBR, original thought is almost imperceptible compared to the noise in our modern day environment.

Universal Consciousness is the gift without which you could never be aware of these insights in the first place. Consciousness is the very principle that allows you to focus your thoughts to create your results into your life. In your victim mindset, you created your depressing results in life all along. The truth is that you have always created your results in life, ever since you became conscious shortly after your birth.

You simply never knew it before. Of course, back then, you most likely created fantastic, positive, happy results because you were an emotionally blank canvas. The truth is that you were born with the divine gift of perfect mental health. This has always been innate within you. But because of your years of conditioning by the society you were brought up in, you simply forgot it.

You were designed from birth simply to feel good. This is your only purpose in life. To feel good, receive inspiration, and share it with others to connect with them and also the environment around you. You knew it when you were an infant before you were influenced by adult humans in this world. All the adult influence and the rules of society and education and years of life experience made you forget. Right now, it might seem impossible for you to feel like that again. But I promise you, you can, and when you are able to drop your ego and live in that good feeling of childlike optimism and enthusiasm for anything and everything, that's when you'll live free and easy and profoundly in your purpose. And it will feel good!

Follow the Good Feeling

This *Good Feeling* is felt deep within your soul and it will be unmistakeable when it manifests for you. Analogous to eating food, there are different types of "good" feeling food. Consider the difference between a fast food meal and a good, healthy home-cooked meal. The fast food option has been designed by the major chains to appeal to your senses all the way from the advertising and packaging down to the look of the food, the smell and the taste. You know it isn't healthy, but sometimes, you don't care because it tastes so good and it really hits the spot. Fast food has been designed to raise your feel-good hormones unnaturally high and the "good" feeling you get from it is short-term and empty in the long run.

Now compare this with the goodness of a healthy home-cooked meal, prepared with love, care, and attention for each ingredient. The preparation, chopping, and cooking is a mindful experience that takes time and effort. The whole process is a full bandwidth sensorial experience ranging from visually inspecting the food to the touch, smells, and taste as well as the sounds of the cooking. Throughout the process, each of these aspects evolve from fresh to the final cooked meal. Then, you sit down to eat and the meal tastes good.

In this example, the "good" feeling includes the mindful aspect of the preparation of the meal. Even if you don't feel it in the preparation, as long as you know how to prepare it, the meal will always be much more nourishing for your body and it will give you a deeper level of satisfaction than the fast food option. This sense of "good" feeling is more wholesome in comparison to the fast-food feeling. If going with your head is like fast food, then going with your heart is wholesome.

The *Good Feeling* you get from following your heart and truly embracing your purpose is a different level entirely, simply because you feel it beyond the physical plane of your body. You feel it in your soul. The fast food "good" is the equivalent to feeling good in your ego and this is unsustainable. You agree with me on some level already and that's why you have read this far.

When you lead your life following the *Good Feeling,* every event becomes a sublime experience. Every interaction contains an opportunity for growth and life in general feels more abundant. You become emotionally bulletproof as you can simply observe others' emotions instead of taking them on for yourself. You find it easier to let go of any negative thinking that pops up and easier to focus on what's here, right now, in this very moment. As the name suggests, you live full of the *Good Feeling*—you naturally smile a lot more. A *lot* more! And rather unsurprisingly, you become a more attractive personality. People want to be with you and they want your time. Opportunities simply present themselves like they never really did before. You love life and you live with full understanding that life loves you right back. Follow the *Good Feeling.* And then pass it on and circulate it.

CHAPTER 8

Powered By The Universe

Human history in a nutshell

Wise people throughout the ages have looked to Nature for inspiration and meaning. Before language, there were cave paintings depicting the forms of Nature in some kind of observation or communication of ideas or artistic expression. There were also tribal dances and rituals, perhaps, to show gratitude for Nature's resources like food and shelter or as a form of prayer to a higher power for more of these resources such as rain. As speech developed, so too did these dances and rituals. They now contained songs as elders communicated stories of life's lessons to the younger generations. As the tribes developed, they each formed their cultural heritage—a culmination of their wisdom passed down through generations, all told through emotional and metaphorical expressions of art.

As language became more complex, the tribes grew more intelligent. They developed tools and agriculture and they survived longer and longer. They grew in numbers and strength and so did their territories, and they became technologically more and more advanced. Before long, they began to find other tribes and then there were wars for territory as they competed for Nature's resources. As time progressed and civilisation dawned, tribal society became more modern as countries and empires were born. New resources were discovered in foreign lands, some more precious than others like gold and diamonds. The more powerful countries invaded, divided, and conquered, extracting and consuming these valuable resources for their own good. The human structures of law, politics, and economics became prominent as trade and commerce became the ways of modern society. Culture developed into religions, popular media and the arts, and technology developed into engineering and science.

The people of the developed nations became comfortable as we lived happily shielded from the elements with an abundance of convenient food all regular shapes and colours and neatly packaged as we became more and more detached from Nature. We developed science in order to be able to empirically measure our reality and to inform us of what is safe and what is not as we developed a distrust of living by feeling. Now, in the modern day in the developed nations, we live busy corporate lifestyles more detached from Nature than in connection with it. Most people are unhappy although they put a brave face on it—their mask. But deep down, they want to escape into their soap operas or computer games or drink or drugs or Friday nights, etc. Most people live to earn barely enough money to survive and secure a reasonably comfortable retirement, resigned to the prospect of a few all right years and whole lot of medical bills as old-age-related diseases take hold.

Where life was once simple and our ancestors were grateful to simply flow with Nature, we now live to escape our manmade hell that we were born into that is anything but what Nature intended for us. As man has made "progress," man has become more and more disconnected from our vital source. You only have to look at the damage we have done to our Earth and that we continue to do for confirmation of this. If you are willing to take responsibility for it, that is.

The Wisdom that has always been there

Like Steve Jobs said, "You can't connect the dots looking forwards; you can only connect the dots looking backwards. So you have to trust that the dots will somehow connect in your future." By now, you have experienced pivotal moments in your life where you made a shift into a new way of thinking and life moved forwards from there. There are experiences in life you are thankful for—the challenges you overcame and the lessons you learnt which all led to the place you are today, to the "you" you are today. Your life history is your treasure trove—your divine gift. There is so much inside you and inside your experience to unpick, and here is one of the first little nuggets that you were ever exposed to:

> *Row, row, row your boat,*
> *Gently down the stream,*
> *Merrily, merrily, merrily, merrily,*
> *Life is but a dream!*

This nursery rhyme which you have known since you were a baby, and possibly while you were in the womb, contains all the wisdom you ever needed to know about life. Ironically, the chances are the person who taught you this rhyme has probably never consciously understood the deeper meaning contained within. They found comfort in it—a heartfelt feeling, it stuck with them, and when they sang it to you, it felt good and right to them to do so.

Before you were born, you were in your mother's womb, and before that, you were not even conceived. You were one with Nature and the Universe and you will be again when your time in this life is up. Your human experience is merely a vessel in which you travel through life.

Your life takes place in a fractal Universe of infinite energy, of electrons flying around atomic nuclei, of planets flying around stars, of galaxies circling each other in the great cosmic dance. The patterns in the Universe repeat themselves at every scale. And just like these structures spin around each other, so too do these same spinning vortex patterns manifest in our Earth's weather and oceans. Similarly, in life, you will seem to experience the same trials over and over again. The details are different but the patterns are recognisable each time. Think about it.

In the rhyme, the stream is the Universe flowing through time. The boat is your vessel that carries you down the stream. The "you" in your vessel is your conscious ego self. You are simply carried along the stream in your boat and you have the ability to row. If you are like most people, you tend to fight the natural flow of the Universe. The Universe carries you one way, but you want to backtrack up the stream to the place you once knew. Notice how the rhyme says to row your boat down the stream? If you are stuck in life, then by definition, you are not in flow. Are you trying to backtrack or hold your position in some way?

The Universe flows of its own accord. This doesn't mean

you can't pick your own direction in life. You have the paddles of your free will, of course, but changing tack is supposed to be hard. And over time, a narrow baby stream becomes a wide forceful torrent of a river and you might feel that the older and more established you are, the harder it is to change course and navigate to your will. But you can if you have the right resolve.

And the right resolve is simply to be merry about it. Life is life. You are of the Universe and the Universe simply flows. There are always things to be happy about and things to be sad about. As discussed at the beginning of the book, you are naturally geared to feel pain more significantly than pleasure in your life. This comes from your animal nature from which you evolved, but you also have the human faculty of choice. You can always choose to look on the bright side of life, no matter how impossible the challenge you are facing seems. You can always choose to be grateful for what life doles up and take responsibility for it. Keeping a positive, joyous mindset, especially in the toughest times, can only make you more creative in your outlook. If the Universe is throwing up a challenge right now, wouldn't a creative, playful, merry outlook help to you create a new result for you?

As you have already learnt, your life as you think it has happened up to now is all an illusion. Life really is but a dream. You are mostly unconscious and only a tiny part of you is conscious when you are awake. Your unconscious is the creative problem-solving part of you, and given that you can choose what to be conscious of, you might as well choose to enjoy what is rather than what isn't. Look for joy in what is and be happy!

Electrify your Magnet

If you spend most of your waking life not enjoying the things that you do or feeling unfulfilled, you are unhappy and you really ought to be doing something else. If you have read this book, you probably already know that. If you have read through the whole content and not simply skipped forward to this section, you'll have learnt a lot about how your mind, body, and soul work. If you feel unfulfilled, your heart—your spiritual compass—is in pain. Your sole purpose in this existence to feel good and it's your heart that tells you when you are on the right track.

When you feel good, you naturally feel grateful, inspired, and fulfilled and you brim over with it—you can't help but want to guide others to their true path also. It's all part of your purpose to feel good in your heart. But it's hard to extract yourself from your current ties of your ego so you'll most likely want to steer away from it. Although this might seem easier, the longer you live off purpose the more it pains your heart. This means you have to have the *courage* to take responsibility and accept the Universe's challenge to overcome it rather than rebounding off it and back into the comfort zone of what you know. If this statement feels like a challenge in itself, then guess what?—this may be your first challenge! Your challenges are reflections of your limiting beliefs and these will continue to show up until you learn the resources to get over them, at which point, you will again feel grateful inspired and fulfilled and make further progress in the right direction.

Key to taking responsibility is to be grateful for that which is a blessing in your life. Even if you are feeling particularly challenged right now, then just the awareness of this is something to be grateful for. Think about your current situation—in what way can you see it as something to be grateful for?

The way you express your *gratitude* to the Universe can take many forms, but it is emotional and requires you to love and respect yourself and others. Gratitude, at its highest level, is to share your divine gift for the benefit of others in the spirit of true service for the progression of mankind in this reality. Your being is designed to receive inspiration from the Universe and convert it into communicable thoughts for the benefit of others. Thus, you speak your inspired thoughts into being and you are a bridge between the spiritual and the real.

Now, of course, you have an ego and a free will, and you can choose to live purely for your ego-felt pleasures. But if you live only to serve your own ego, you block the flow of your inspiration from birthing into this reality. You'll feel good to an extent, but this will be short-lived and leave you chasing for more. This is not to say your ego doesn't deserve to feel good—it most definitely does and you have to feel rewarded, but this is only the foundation for that real wholesome feeling that comes from your heart when you serve your soul!

This level of feeling good is to the level of feeling worthy. *Worthiness* is a high vibration state where you already own the result. You simply know the Universe has the result waiting in store for you and you are on the right path to attract it to you. This is that feeling of being magnetised to your chosen destiny. You have successfully paddled your rowboat into the right stream.

You don't control the flow of the Universe. You can only finesse your path through it toward the goal you want. This means you have to have *faith* that the Universe will carry you there. This leap of faith is a challenge in itself and the Universe will test you—Do you really want your goal enough that you'll hold on for dear faith? Again, you have to have tremendous courage to own up to the fact that you willed yourself to this point and take responsibility for choosing this future and steering toward it in the first place. This might take exceptional commitment and dedication to persevere through the hardest of times, to *know* that you will claim that prize that you are worthy of.

You must *let go* of the anchors that hold you back and prevent you from flowing through the Universe to your destination. This means learning to consciously *forgive* the negative actions of others to recover your jovial sense of flow again. Your ego may have been bruised but this is the lesser part of you and will quickly heal over if you give it the opportunity. Also, you must *detach* from your goal and put it to the back of your mind. You know the result you want and how it feels, but you have to create space for the Universe to manifest it for you. Nature abhors a vacuum and requires time, space, and energy to work to fill it and that will happen when the time is right and you have taken enough purposeful actions toward it.

Lastly, you must be *consistent* in how you care for your consciousness. You must *focus* on that which makes your heart sing whenever you can. Follow the good feeling. To do this, you have to maintain an open mind. Throughout this book, you have learnt about the divine equipment you have been blessed with—your human experience of life—and you have learned how you have been creating your reality all along. You have been introduced to various models, frameworks, and techniques to understand your level of awareness and to be able to take charge of it. Learn to master your thoughts. Develop, practice, and internalise the italicised qualities in this section of the book

Wherever you are in your journey right now, know that you are in the right place for you and have faith that the right things are happening for you to *take responsibility for your purpose in life*. Just by reading this book, you have taken your first step already, so congratulations—you are on the right path! In this book, I have outlined the concepts required for you to live your best life, Powered by the Universe and magnetised to your best results. Thank you for reading this book and remember to look beyond my words for the underlying meaning. If you would like to learn to master your thoughts and take practical steps toward a better future, then go to www.PoweredByTheUniverseBook.com now for your next steps and some valuable free bonuses!

Acknowledgements

There are so many people I wish to thank for their impact on my life. I have come to believe we each are a universe of experience bumping into each other and merging in time-bound ways like bubbles floating around in a great spiritual multi-verse. For those of you that have actually met me you know I don't mind being considered somewhat eccentric!

First and foremost I thank my parents for the secure environment you brought me up in. I am so blessed to have been gifted you, for all your devotion and absolute unconditional fierce love. I have met so many people in my life and I appreciate how truly blessed I am for having been born to you. Although we had many challenges, I understand why now.

And of course to my big sister Helen—we're not so in contact these days but I love you so much! You really came to my aid when it most counted by helping to fund my coaching training. Shortly after that was the first time I consciously witnessed a miracle of circumstances simply appear in my life, out of the ether, effortlessly fitting the specification I needed at that specific time in life. Also without knowing it, you started me on this path recommending books like Sophie's

World and Zen and the Art of Motorcycle Maintenance. And although you don't remember it I distinctly remember childhood conversations questioning our reality like, "How do I know that what I see as the colour red, you don't see as the colour blue?" This is really where it started for me. Thank you!

Of course I have to thank my school teachers and my school friends. Also my family friends—big up to the BDMA massiv with whom we had so much fun at each other's houses playing football and team hide and seek—how brilliant a time of life that was and how lucky we were! And my 6th form friends—what a treasure trove of hilarity! OMG we had some ridiculous and downright dangerous times but I remember it all so fondly. You have all contributed so much to the foundation of my character and I thank you so much!

And who would I be without my university friends and of course my bandmates and everyone involved with Tessellators and Hundred Handed over the years. You guys have provided so much fun and laughter in my life—in many ways you're my reference point for how life is supposed to feel! I am indebted to you forever. Thank you!

To all of my tenants and lodgers over the years, thank you for sharing the journey in the ways you did. Between you, you've seen almost all sides of me.

Marica you would not believe the impact our relationship has had on my life and still does—I am so grateful for this most important reference point in my life.

To Master Richard Hamlin I heard philosophy in your lessons as much as I did of Tai Chi. Your teachings underpin pretty much everything I do in life in some way or another as I build my foundations first and then the house on top.

As much as I talk about the innate unhealthiness of the corporate environment I am greatly indebted to everyone that has ever employed me. The LBI massiv—what an amazing time that was! And a special mention has to go to Steve Oram and Keith Hill from my GTCE days—you really looked after me and helped me to grow.

I wish to acknowledge anyone in my life that has shown up in some form that was difficult for me to handle at all. Without the experiences we shared I could not have grown into the person I am today so I am full of love and gratitude for you. Whatever the situation that happened between us in life, it simply had to happen in that way for us both to grow. Thank you.

And of course I have to thank all the healers who ever picked up the pieces when I was a mess. Sherry White and Daisy Nokes you both really proved to me against my science trained mind that there really are healing truths beyond the reach of the science I studied. The healing experiences I had with you profoundly impacted my life and provide important reference points in life for me. Dr Gino Amato you were the first NHS doctor I experienced with an artful approach to medicine—I don't know what the state of my skin would be in today if I hadn't have met you when I did.

David Key—it's all in a day work for you to profoundly change people's lives. You can never know just how grateful I am for all you have taught me of NLP and the Three Principles and for your incredible compassion when it came to the crunch. If you didn't help me when you did I might never have learned to have faith in the way I can now, so thank you.

To Morty Lefkoe—I never knew you and you died very

shortly after I discovered your online course. I'm so grateful or the legacy you left which released much for me and inspires me to leave similar resources in my wake.

I'd also like to thank Nicole Daedone for your most amazing coaching model and the practice that came with it which brought me so much healing for my Desire, for my connection with Nature and consciousness of my inner feminine and masculine.

To Eric Ho and Vishal Morjaria I'm super grateful for your spirituality, your knowledge and practical business coaching. I've experienced some profound shifts at your events and through your coaching. You both are a source of much magic for me. I am grateful to you both and also to Success Resources, Marcus De Maria and Luca Lorenzoni—I am so grateful for your training organisations and the work you do worldwide to free so many people around the world from their limited thinking. You inspire me.

And I have to thank Richard Bandler and John Grinder for your creation of Neuro-Linguistic Programming which has given me that framework for understanding my mind and communicability, which really enabled me to recover from my depression and help others too. Your work has proven to be invaluable in the personal development space and I can't wait for more people in the world to wake up to these essential tools for navigating and directing the mind. I also want to give special thanks to Paul R Scheele for your Ultimate You Library of hypnosis audios which have really improved my life in many turbulent times over the years.

To the huge superstar coaches and influencers operating today like Tony Robbins, Bob Proctor, T Harv Eker, Marie Diamond, Les Brown, Grant Cardone, Gary Vaynerchuk etc—In most cases, I have never met you but your influences on me whether directly or indirectly through your reputation have been especially profound and I am deeply grateful for the wisdom you continue to put out for the benefit of humanity.

To the authors living and deceased that have most impacted my life and philosophy including Jostein Gaarder, Robert Pirsig, Gabrielle Bernstein, Tim Ferriss to name but a tiny few, thank you for the knowledge you have passed on to me and the future generations of mankind.

And I am so grateful for the influences of Wayne Dyer, Sydney Banks and Napoleon Hill. Without question the great spiritual truth has always been available, passed down through the great figures of world's religions and the ancients before them, for all of whom I also give thanks. Thanks to the likes of you and the generations of coaches, consultants and trainers that came before you, these lessons are preserved.

And finally I give my greatest thanks to Nature and the Universe and for my growing consciousness of it all. I love my life, I love my thoughts, I love my friends and I love you. Thank you.

Printed in Poland
by Amazon Fulfillment
Poland Sp. z o.o., Wrocław